Praise for *Writing in the Sand*

"Thomas Moore's groundbreaking reinterpretation of the Gospels shines a new light on the profound teachings of Jesus. Through his study of some of the most pertinent passages in the Bible, Moore offers readers a long-awaited, modern, practical application of the scripture, and illustrates the 21st-century relevance of Jesus' visionary philosophy."

— **Deepak Chopra**, author of
The Third Jesus: The Christ We Cannot Ignore
and *Jesus: A Story of Enlightenment*

"Thomas Moore sets out to reveal the secret of who the real Jesus was. In doing so, he resurrects the deep Joy of the Gospels and brings their true meaning to life. Hallelujah!"

— **Robert Holden, Ph.D.**, author of
Be Happy and *Happiness NOW!*

"Thomas Moore provides a fresh description of Jesus that is both compelling and provocative. By focusing on his humanity, Moore introduces us to a Jesus who radically challenges our understanding of how to live in meaningful community. At a time when we face unprecedented economic, political, and environmental problems, this may be Moore's most important book. It is not for the faint of heart. If he is right, we must drastically change how we think and act."

— **James D. Guy, Jr., Ph.D.**, clinical psychologist and
president & founder, Headington Institute

"In this powerful book, Thomas Moore uses his transformative soul to unravel for us, people of all faiths, Jesus' wisdom and intellect. This is a fascinating book —an awesome resurrection of the spirit. If you were to read one book in the field of spirituality, read **Writing in the Sand**. *You'll be truly enlightened."*

— **T. Byram Karasu, M.D.**, author of
The Spirit of Happiness

WRITING IN THE SAND

WRITING IN THE SAND

Jesus and the Soul of the Gospels

Thomas Moore

HAY HOUSE, INC.
Carlsbad, California • New York City
London • Sydney • Johannesburg
Vancouver • Hong Kong • New Delhi

Published and distributed in the United States by: Hay House, Inc.: www.hayhouse.com • *Published and distributed in Australia by:* Hay House Australia Pty. Ltd.: www.hayhouse.com.au • *Published and distributed in the United Kingdom by:* Hay House UK, Ltd.: www. hayhouse.co.uk • *Published and distributed in the Republic of South Africa by:* Hay House SA (Pty), Ltd.: www.hayhouse.co.za • *Distributed in Canada by:* Raincoast: www.raincoast.com • *Published in India by:* Hay House Publishers India: www.hayhouse.co.in

Design: Tricia Breidenthal

Library of Congress Cataloging-in-Publication Data

Moore, Thomas.
  Writing in the sand : Jesus and the soul of the Gospels / Thomas Moore. -- 1st ed.
     p. cm.
  Includes bibliographical references.
  ISBN 978-1-4019-2413-3 (hardcover : alk. paper) 1. Jesus Christ--Teachings. I. Title.
  BS2415.M62 2009
  232--dc22

                            2008051457

ISBN: 978-1-4019-2413-3

12 11 10 09 4 3 2 1
1st edition, May 2009

Printed in the United States of America

To the men and women
of the Servite Community,
who gave me my foundation.

CONTENTS

Introduction   xi

CHAPTER 1   A New Way of Imagining Human Life   1

CHAPTER 2   A Radical Shift in Vision   21

CHAPTER 3   Water to Wine   33

CHAPTER 4   Love in the Kingdom   45

CHAPTER 5   Everyone a Healer   59

CHAPTER 6   Face Your Demons   75

CHAPTER 7   Transfiguration and Metamorphosis   91

CHAPTER 8   Reinventing the Ego   105

CHAPTER 9   Mary Magdalen, Whom He Loved   125

CHAPTER 10   Come Out, Lazarus   137

CHAPTER 11   The Joys of Earthly Existence   149

Conclusion   163

Acknowledgments   169

Endnotes   171

About the Author   179

INTRODUCTION

People are often astonished that a simple man in a remote time and place gave rise to a worldwide religion and attracted millions of followers. But what is really astonishing is his dream for humanity. The splendor of Saint Peter's Basilica is nothing compared to the hope and promise of the alternative way of life Jesus envisioned. This book presents the essence of that teaching and offers a way of understanding it intelligently and devotedly in the 21st century.

Jesus was a sophisticated man who lived simply, walking from town to town, healing and comforting, while espousing a spiritual philosophy that has yet to be fully appreciated and understood. He lived in primitive times compared to our own, but his thinking was more advanced than ours. I suspect that our tendency to sentimentalize him or turn him into a moral crusader is a defense against the sheer radical challenge of his intellect. As long as we piously enshrine his personality, we don't have to feel the full force of his vision for humanity.

Of all those who have commented on him, Oscar Wilde may have been the most perceptive. He saw in Jesus someone who could transcend the splitting of good and evil and light and shadow, and therefore avoid the pitfall of moralism—the bad habit of making simple judgments of right and wrong. "His primary desire was not to reform people," Wilde wrote, "any more than his primary desire was to relieve suffering. To turn an interesting thief into a tedious honest man was not his aim."[1]

People often ask me, what is the goal of caring for your soul? I say it isn't health or being on the right side or even doing good and avoiding evil. It is to live an interesting and worthwhile life and help others do the same. This is perhaps what Oscar Wilde meant. Jesus wasn't a bland moralist offering pie-in-the-sky rewards for good living; he was a sophisticated man living the good life of friends, loves, community, and a fascinating, original philosophy.

In this book I want to show how challenging Jesus' teachings are, in a way far different from the moral coaching associated with him, and how to live the way of life he spelled out. In some ways the picture I present is a completely new Jesus, a figure I believe any 21st-century person could adopt as a focus for a vibrant and intelligent spiritual life, one that doesn't defend itself against the shadow elements. The Gospels present a vision so radical that people have been intimidated by it. For centuries it has been kept hidden beneath thick layers of moral, theological, and devotional camouflage. This book is an unveiling, a revelation, and a resurrection.

Gospels

Since I am writing this book for people of all faiths, including those who may be more interested in spirituality than in religion, I will begin with a few facts about the Gospels.

The Gospels are "sacred texts" that tell the story of Jesus, his life, teachings, death, and resurrection. The word *gospel* means "good news" and is a translation of the Greek word for these writings, *euangelon. Eu* means "good" and *angelon* means "message." The Gospels are a good message in the sense that the reader can be happy to find a story that will give meaning to his life.

Euangelon shifts easily into the English word *evangelist,* which first referred to the authors of the four canonical Gospels, Mark, Matthew, Luke, and John. Later, people who promoted the ideas in the Gospels were called evangelists. People who want to live the Gospel message closely call themselves evangelicals.

In the first centuries after Jesus, communities dedicated to his spirituality came up with many gospels, stories, and teachings that portrayed the essence of the Jesus way; each with its own emphasis. Today, for instance, scholars talk about the Thomas community that evolved the Gospel of Thomas and the John community that created the Gospel of John. Many of these so-called non-canonical Gospels—those that didn't make it into the final list approved in the 5th century—are appearing in English translation today and are of interest to many because of the fuller picture of the teachings that they offer.

But the four basic Gospels of Mark, Luke, Matthew, and John form the core of the New Testament. Other writings in that collection are stories of the community around Jesus right after his death, letters of theology and spiritual practice from Paul and others, and the mystical Book of Revelations of John.

On the surface, the Gospels may give the impression that they are history or chronicle, just as we might write history today. But a closer look shows that they are more complicated. They involve teachings, parables, stories of a holy teacher, wondrous events such as magical healings, and, of course, resurrection from death. They are not history in our sense of the word as much as theology.

The basic Gospels were written in Greek, and over the centuries scholars have studied every word and every nuance. Existing manuscripts take us back only to the 4th century, so many conclusions about the Gospels come from study of the texts as literary forms.

Today there is some tension between scholars and followers. Scholars emphasize the deep spiritual truths expressed in various literary ways. Followers worry that something essential is lost in all the scholarship. They particularly dislike any effort to downplay the factual element and reduce all the stories and images to metaphor.

In this book, I admire and rely on the work of scholars, but I also appreciate the followers' desire to find direct inspiration for a life-giving spirituality. So I avoid both the rationalism of the scholars and the literalism of the followers. I find myself somewhere in between.

At the top of my agenda in this book is to recover the Gospels from the trend among scholars to get caught up in history and among followers to interpret these precious texts literally and moralistically. Having studied several world religions closely, I find the Gospels similar in some ways to other sacred texts. They are subtle and profound. To turn them into simplistic guidelines that provide an escape from the complexities that face us is an affront to their depth.

I am writing as someone who has the highest respect for the Gospels as spiritual literature. I see no reason to say that they are better or more important than the Buddhist sutras or the Vedas or Greek tragedies or Native American ritual songs, all of which are holy texts. The Gospels are especially important to me because I was born and raised in a Catholic family. In a profound way, they are the innate source of my spirituality.

I would like to show people of other traditions, those who have abandoned the Christian way, and those who have no spiritual allegiances how valuable these texts are for all of us. You don't have to be a believer to be a follower. You don't have to be Christian to make the Gospels an important source of your spiritual life and practice. You only have to read these texts for their spiritual insight and for the spiritual path they offer.

Gospel Decline

In recent decades people have reacted to the dominance of science and the formalities of religious institutions by turning away from Christianity and going to exotic spiritual traditions and teachers. Many are abandoning the Gospels because they are tired of male-dominated authority, feelings of guilt, and an absence of spiritual guidance. Before, they enjoyed certainty in theological matters and the security of an unchanging tradition. Now, they are out on the road experimenting and exploring.

I run into people today who say they used to be Christian and loved the Gospels, but now they don't see their relevance. They aren't challenged. They wonder if there is any spirituality in the Gospels or if they are useful only for morals, rules, and beliefs. They are becoming Buddhists and Sufis, or joining spiritual communities. I hope this book will offer these people a way to reimagine the rich stories and imagery of the Gospels, find spiritual meaning in them, and perhaps gain a new kind of certainty and stability. The Gospels are easily as rich and challenging as any other spiritual source.

There are two ways to be spiritually secure: One is to attach to a fixed and uncomplicated teaching, leadership, and set of moral standards. Another is to be open to life, ever deepening your understanding and giving up all defensiveness around your convictions. Jesus represents this second approach. The first way offers only the illusion of certainty, an illusion that must be maintained by anxious inflexibility. Jesus' way is to live from a deeper source, with values that cannot be codified in a list of rules. Central among his values is love, understood as profound respect for the other.

As I write this book, an image keeps coming to mind: Jesus in the tomb, not yet resurrected, sealed off by huge, heavy stones. Though the Gospels tell the story of his rising from the tomb, Jesus has yet to be resurrected as a cultural force and a model for living a life of values and intelligence. His importance does not come from creating a church or a theology, not even a religion. He embodies a new way of dealing with conflict, a new level of mutual understanding and forgiveness, and a new, more subtle and more flexible notion of ethics and morality.

Jesus is so effectively sealed off in the tomb of misunderstanding that to know him now you have to know the secret core of his vision. You need a key to gain entry into the world he revealed as a concrete possibility, a utopia of sorts, a world where human beings could thrive.

The Secret of the Gospels

This book attempts to reveal the secret of who Jesus was and offers several keys to open the door to his vision. As we'll see, the secret is there in the name Christ. It is hidden in the original-language versions of Gospel passages that millions of people know by heart in the vernacular. It is hidden in the teachings of many world religions, only waiting to be applied to the Gospels. It is hidden in every parable and teaching, but people miss it because they are not looking for it or because they have never stopped to think beyond what they were taught as children.

Certain key words in the Gospels can reveal this secret but only if you read the words carefully and with an open mind. When you reach the end of this book, after exploring the many facets and intricate subplots of the Gospels, you should know this secret thoroughly.

My method is quite simple: I read the words of the Gospels without the cautionary voice of authority or tradition telling me what they mean. I free myself from centuries of interpretations and habits of thought and translation. But I read these subtle texts in an educated way. I look at the rich history of the Greek words, including older, classical meanings. I read the works of authors who have studied the texts without being overly influenced by creeds and traditions. I apply contemporary ideas from depth psychology and literature, and I use my knowledge of the world's religions. The result is a fresh way of understanding who Jesus was and what he was trying to do.

I bring my background with me, of course. I've devoted my life to the study of theology, world religions, the history of art, depth psychology—Jungian and archetypal psychology especially—and world mythology. In all my writing, I stress the origins of words and the many levels of meaning in stories and images. I look for insight rather than fact and nuance rather than definitive interpretations. I write about the soul, as distinct from the spirit. This is truly a book about the soul—the mysterious depth, not just the shining spirit—of the Gospels.

I explore the deeper significance of the language rather than accept traditional translations because they're traditional. Usually, traditional means unconscious—we may not have thought much about important words that we use as the basis for our spirituality. I understand the concern of more orthodox Christians about people going into flights of fancy about etymologies and meanings, but that doesn't mean we can't open our minds to the rich heritage of language.

Even though I propose a fresh reading of the Gospels, I don't question the reality of Jesus or whisk away the essence of the Gospels in metaphor and psychology. On the contrary, I see the Gospels as an intelligent and profound source of insight into the essential problems of the human race. They are not so radically different from other spiritual writings of the world—in them I see shades of the shaman, Sufi humor and mysticism, the everyday holiness of the ancient Greeks, and, of course, Jewish piety and wisdom. I have called myself a "Zen Catholic," and I also see the Zen spirit in many passages from the Gospels.

I wouldn't like to see Buddhists spend their energy defending the historical existence of the Buddha at the expense of his teaching and the beautiful stories about him. I feel the same about Jesus. I can ignore the history question and focus on deepening our understanding of his teachings and the rich stories we have about him.

Therefore, this is a book about Jesus that brackets out Christianity. To get to the crux of the Gospels, generally I have to abandon established readings and tread on pieties that are taken for granted as valuable and revered. I have no intention of leading the reader to an appreciation of Christian tradition but rather to an appreciation of the Gospels as they are liberated from tradition.

Jesus described himself as a visitor to earth bringing a life-saving message. In this he resembles a figure from certain Gnostic stories who comes to earth on a mission. He has something of immense importance to say, something precious—like a pearl, the Gnostics say—that has been forgotten. (We see that on more than one occasion Jesus referred to himself as a pearl.) Jesus also seems to be part shaman, a person who lives in several dimensions and brings his vision to us who live on the surface.

In the case of a shaman, you wouldn't want to honor the person as much as the vision he has received on his spiritual journeys. With Jesus, too, an emphasis on his person may weaken his message. We may spend more energy deifying and championing him than trying to live the way of life he so carefully spelled out.

This book builds chapter by chapter in search of the secret of who Jesus was and how best to live his teachings. I am not a New Testament scholar, and so I rely on the work of the specialists. But I offer my own carefully considered translations and interpretations of what the stories and teachings mean. Layer upon layer of narrative and teaching will reveal the basics of a special spirituality taken from the Gospels.

The Visitor

When I was 10 years old I saw the sci-fi film *The Day the Earth Stood Still*. It's about a man who comes to Earth in a spaceship to tell the warring governments of Earth not to bring their conflicts out into space. Like a Gnostic messenger, he travels here to warn human beings to change their way of life.

This movie version of what was a short story consciously draws parallels to the story of Jesus. I have always been inspired by the movie, but I would rather bring its spirit of renewal to our understanding of Jesus than see Christ themes in the film. The point of Jesus' mission is not to draw attention to himself but to transform the way human beings live.

Breaking free of reasonable, standard, but unconscious patterns of thought is what Jesus was about. It's as though he descended from another planet to tell us where we are going wrong and how our basic assumptions are off base. That is why we are so caught up in wars and injustice and inequalities. We assume that these gaps in human intelligence are natural and inevitable. Jesus talks as a visitor unfamiliar with this reasoning and offers a way out of our stupidity. He assumes that we don't have to live with wary paranoia, demonic violence, and self-destructive narcissism—three kinds of personal and cultural neurosis that threaten our existence.

In an often-quoted Sufi story, a holy man is found crawling on the ground at night under a beam of light. "Are you looking for something?" someone asks. "Yes," he says, "a key." "Where did you lose it?" He points into the darkness. "Over there." "Then why are you looking here?" "Because this is where the light is."

I used to think of this story as a joke about how we tend to avoid the darkness and stay in the light of understanding. Now, after studying many Sufi stories, I think differently. The holy man was breaking free of the reasoning that says you should look for what is lost where you think you lost it—especially the key to your existence. He wasn't foolish at all. He was simply free of the conventional and the obvious.

In spiritual matters, generally we need to bring all our intelligence to bear on creating a vision of reality and a way of life. In relation to the Gospels, we should also be as intelligent and open-minded as possible, receiving their message as a challenge to our lazy habits of thought. The world is in a tragic state, getting worse rather than better, and yet we often escape into sentimental spiritualities that give us an illusion of peace and harmony that has no relation to the facts. Think of the Gospels as having a subtle intelligence and complexity, offering a way to make sense of life and save us from the neurosis and anxiety that make us aggressive and narcissistic. Think of the Gospels as a source of healing, something to help make a world community in place of a planet of competitors and enemies.

This book offers a view of Jesus that is positive and yet different from the standard one. It reveals a Jesus whose teaching is for anyone in search of meaning, not just Christians. It shows a Gospel message that belongs to no church or community or tradition. It suggests that Jesus' purpose was not to form a religion but to transform the world, not to exploit this life for a heavenly reward but to establish heaven on earth.

CHAPTER 1

A NEW WAY OF IMAGINING HUMAN LIFE

The Central Image of Kingdom

As you travel around, let people know that the kingdom of heaven has come. Take care of the sick, waken the lifeless, get to the root of suffering, and banish the demonic.

—MATTHEW 10:7–8

"Kingdom of heaven"—this image is the heart and soul of the Gospels. You will find it woven into all the stories and teachings. It is so central that your interpretation of "kingdom" will determine how you respond to the deep mystery presented everywhere in these texts.

Some think of the kingdom as the afterlife, some as a church, but I see nothing in the Gospels to support either view. Jesus talks about the kingdom as being within you and in your midst. The passage from Matthew above makes it clear that you reveal the kingdom

by the way you live and act—not that you live morally
and virtuously but that you work at healing, wakening,
caring for, and calming others.[2]

The Language of Parables

Jesus never describes the kingdom so directly that
you have a clear idea of it. Rather, he uses parables and
allusions to suggest what it is like. But why would he be
so indirect? If "kingdom" is such an important idea, why
not speak plainly about what it is and what it means?
Some say that his use of parables is a cultural trait, a
custom of his time and place, but in such an important
matter we need a more substantial reason.

Like all fiction and poetry, parables convey subtle
insights that can't be expressed in plain language. Parables could help us think more deeply and grasp the
mystery in the idea of the kingdom. They tell something
positive and at the same time confuse, because they are
conveying paradoxical ideas. They have to conceal the
mysteries at the same time that they reveal them.

A parable is a parabola: you go far out into a story,
make a U-turn, and then come back with a surprising
twist. All the Gospel parables have this twist that upsets
your logic and your habits of thinking. Their purpose
is first to stun you and then to take advantage of your
disequilibrium to propose an outrageous possibility.
Worldly wisdom would never get you to the Jesus worldview. You can't condense it into a rational idea.

If you read Jesus as a moral teacher, you try to live
a better life, but you don't change your basic understanding of what life is all about. This is the plain

vanilla approach to Jesus: live a good life. I prefer the spice approach, catching the subtle humor, the biting paradox, and even sometimes the absurdity. These turn your mind upside down and inside out—the only way to freshen your imagination.

One of the lessons I learned while practicing therapy is the importance of wit and a certain kind of irony and an appreciation for the absurd things that happen in life. If a person is zealous, not just about religion but about everything in life, he is easily thrown into deep confusion and depression. I have worked with people who were labeled psychotic, and I thought that there was hope for them when they could laugh at the contradictions in their lives.

People in therapy tell straightforward stories about their lives, often to convince you or themselves of their usual way of understanding it all. But if their story turns on them and becomes a parable, or if they look at a dream that is full of puzzles, they can no longer hang onto the story that has kept them stuck for years.

The same is true of the spiritual life. If we are zealots, passionate about the way we have found to make sense of life and dismissive of other ways, or if we don't see how complex life is and are not prepared to forgive ourselves and others for mistakes, then our spirituality is in danger of being neurotic, easily threatened and therefore excessively defended.

The failure to appreciate the radical nature of Jesus' teaching may account for the lack of excitement and challenge in many churches. You participate in rituals that are far from earth-shaking and listen to sermons that are full of platitudes. Jung said that the Jesus community has been turned into a "misery institute." Certainly it often takes the pleasure out of life. But even worse, it has become a "novocaine philosophy," numbing us with the mindless habits of church attendance and the rote learning of meaningless dogmas.

Parables serve the mysteries of the Gospels rather than dispel them in lengthy explanation. Who Jesus was and what the kingdom is all about are not exactly problems in need of a solution. Who was the historical Jesus? Was he married or celibate? Where did he study? These are interesting questions, but they distract from the mystery. A problem is a challenge to our intelligence that can be solved; a mystery is a reality so deep and subtle that you have to find your way into it and have your life changed by it.

The image of the kingdom is important because it implies a "realm" of meaning different from the usual. It is a "kingdom of heaven" rather than earth, a place of bliss and idealistic values. The Gospels suggest that it's more important to enter that kingdom than to live a good life.

The Shocking Parables

I used to think of the parables as each teaching a moral virtue: you should be kind, unprejudiced, forgiving, and so on. But now I see how they work together to describe the nature of the kingdom. They are not moral lessons; they don't promote the plain vanilla life. Instead, they shock your old patterns of thought so you can imagine a new and vastly more interesting life. It is one thing to try to be a better person and another thing to change the way you think.

Consider this rather unfamiliar parable from the Gospel of Thomas.

> Jesus said: "The kingdom of the father is like a certain woman who was carrying a jar full of meal. While she was walking on the road, still some distance from home, the handle of the jar broke and the meal emptied out behind her on the road. She did not realize it; she had noticed no accident. When she reached her house, she set the jar down and found it empty."
>
> —GOSPEL OF THOMAS 97

In a sense, the kingdom we are talking about is empty. "Empty" here doesn't mean worthless; it means not fully visible and concrete, like a church or a belief system. It is more an attitude toward life than a religious institution, more a quality of mind than a formal church. You don't necessarily see it in a church full of people, but it is revealed in one person helping another in need.

In Buddhism, "empty" means not being attached to the language and forms of the religion but living and being in a way spelled out by the Buddha's teaching and example. The Thomas parable implies something similar: You let all your concern about being good, believing the right thing, and using the right language empty out. You let go of all those principles that give life simple meaning, and you are left with the pristine teaching and example of Jesus creating an entirely new way of life. You empty your head of ideas and become a new kind of person. It's a matter of being rather than believing.

Perhaps you can participate in a religion or a church in an "empty" way, but that is difficult. By its very nature, a church focuses on itself, on its rules and dogma, and encourages people to follow rather than to create a new life. Church life might keep the Gospel teaching in mind and help you understand it better. It may motivate you and may help you participate in the mystery through ritual. But it may also get in the way, because the church is not the kingdom.

When you look for the kingdom in a person, you don't look for special clothes or particular words coming out of his mouth. The kingdom is invisible, empty. It's more like a color than an object, more like a sound than a structure. It isn't anything more than a point of view, but it is a perspective on life that makes all the difference. As literalism and hard belief gradually leak out of your idea of the Jesus way, you get closer to the mystery of the kingdom. You come home.

In a typical metaphor for emptiness, the Chinese spiritual classic the *Tao Te Ching* says:

> Cut doors and windows for a room;
> It is the holes which make it useful.[3]

The kingdom, too, is like an open window, nothing in itself, and yet it allows everything. It is transparent and translucent. It allows the fullness of life to shine through. It is a way of seeing and living, but it is not an entity separate from ordinary existence. It is not a set of beliefs as much as a slant on life. In some ways it's a door opening to a new life, but even better, it's a window you can look through and see another world.

In another parable, Jesus says:

> What is the kingdom of God like? What can I compare it to? It's like a mustard seed that a person took and planted in his garden. It grew into a tree, and the birds of the sky made nests in its branches.

> —LUKE 13:18–19

As many commentators point out, Jesus' listeners might have expected him to say that the kingdom is like the great cedars of Lebanon. Instead, it's like a mustard seed, the tiniest of seeds, which becomes a small bush—hardly a good place for birds to make nests. The image is extreme and even comic. It's as though Jesus said, "You think the kingdom is like a huge sequoia tree in a great forest. In fact, it's more like a weed in front of your house, and actually more like a tiny seed from that weed."

This is a hint that the secret we are after, the clue to the meaning of "kingdom" and the general thrust of the Gospels, is small but potent, utterly ordinary and yet transcendent. Like a weed compared to a rose, it is something people would rather not bother with. Not a huge belief system but a slight shift in vision and values, the loss of all your ambitions and cravings changes your world.

Furthermore, as they would on a weed, people will look down on the Gospel way of life. Turning the other cheek is stupid and naïve, they will say. Forgiving people for their sexual mistakes is being permissive and immoral. Followers of Jesus would like his teaching to be like a mighty tree, mirrored in a grand cathedral or the regal trappings of a bishop, but Jesus uses the image of a little bush, a weed. Jesus never looked like the pope; he dressed like a peasant.

At a personal level, I have felt this seed/weed spirituality gradually transforming me throughout my adult life. I started out as a card-carrying poster boy for Christianity. I was an altar boy, a seminarian, a monk, and almost a priest. But today all that highly visible, hardcore Christianity has become a tiny, flexible, lively, breathing spring from which my life flows. But you can hardly see the Gospels in my spirituality. In fact, you can hardly see my spirituality. Tinier than a mustard seed; less noticeable than a weed.

My personal spirituality is not noble and inspiring, and yet to me it is precious. I feel its inferiority, its lowliness, but I know that all these feelings are in tune with the Gospels. The last shall be first. "Let the children come to me," Jesus says.

Jesus himself was a slight figure in the rich cultural and religious life of the 1st century. Today there is little, if any, evidence of his historical existence. The one passage from the Jewish historian Josephus, often used as the final word on Jesus' historical existence, is questionable. Jesus himself is like a mustard seed—hardly visible in the historical record.

Paradoxically, by not making Jesus himself the object of your spiritual devotion, an idol in your spirituality, you allow the kingdom to come to life in you. As your bloated language and too-precious ideals shrink to the size of a mustard seed, you come to life in a new way. Instead of being full of yourself for possessing the truth, you live your life quietly, knowing that you are spiritually alive.

I have never understood why some people promote simply accepting Jesus and stopping there. Inflating Jesus and making little of his radical philosophy makes Jesus too big. He gets in the way of his message. Then the metaphors of weed, seed, and empty jar don't apply. The big Jesus is not consistent with the teaching of the parables.

The Zen teacher Shunryu Suzuki said that Zen Buddhism is "nothing special." The same could be applied to Jesus and his way: it is nothing special, and yet it is worth devoting your life to, as Suzuki devoted his to Zen. Some Buddhists say, "If you see the Buddha on the road, kill him." They mean no disrespect, but rather warn against making an idol even of the Buddha himself. It's difficult to imagine a follower of Jesus saying something similar, and yet the empty-jar parable suggests just that.

Sigmund Freud said that when people display something excessively, that display means they lack the very thing they are displaying. A person who acts as if he knows everything may be inwardly worried about his ignorance. When religious people display their faith, one wonders if they are protecting themselves from the lack of it. When the Jesus vision is subtle and transparent, it may be more grounded and sure than when it is shouted in your face. Our parables seem to say that as long as you keep leaking, losing all that substantial stuff that you have been attached to, the kingdom will take shape. Nowhere else in the Gospels does Jesus sound more like a Zen master.

The Kingdom as Myth

The kingdom of God is not arriving in a way you can see directly. Nor will people be able to say, "That's it!" Or "There it is!" The thing is, the kingdom of God is within you.

—LUKE 17:20–21

I would like to say that the kingdom is a new myth of human living, but I'm aware that people often think of myth as something false and fantastic. Those who study religion and culture, on the other hand, use the words *myth* and *mythology* to refer to something more positive and serious. For them, mythology is the story or narrative, sometimes unspoken, by which people find meaning and make sense of their world. When taken seriously, the word *myth* speaks of the very heart of the religious life.

A mythology has two levels: it may be an actual story, like the tales of the Greek gods and goddesses or even the story of Jesus, or it may be a lived story, like the implicit worldview of science that plays a central role in the myth that shapes the modern world. Notice I am making no judgments in my use of the word *myth* but only point to a story, told or lived, that shapes individuals and society. In this sense, to speak of the mythic Jesus takes nothing away from his reality, historicity, and importance.

Joseph Campbell made this meaning popular in his television programs and books, where he spells out four functions or purposes of myth:

> To relate to the mystery of the world in which we live—the religious function.
>
> To create a meaningful understanding of the natural world—the cosmological function.
>
> To establish and maintain values and an ethical way of life—the moral function.
>
> To allow the individual person to live a meaningful life in relation to nature and in society—the psychological function.[4]

In Campbell's sense, Jesus is proposing a new myth to live by, an alternative vision for accomplishing these four goals: to have a spiritual existence, to have an appropriate relationship with the natural world, to live by real communal values, and to be psychologically secure and creative. This vision of a new way of being covers the whole of one's existence. Jesus addresses not only the spiritual and religious dimensions but the whole of life— everything we do.

In the Gospels Jesus clearly distinguishes between legalistic spiritual practice—following the rules, honoring authority, observing traditions—and living with compassion. The old way is one of authoritarianism, guilt, and constraint. The new law, a new way of ordering life, is to honor people not for their position but for their humanity, to serve all people, and to be a healing presence wherever you are. This is clearly how Jesus models human life and how he embodies "the kingdom of heaven." You find the kingdom when you discover a way out of the limited vision given to you by your family and culture, when your old mind has been washed clean, when you accept yourself, when you discover the rewards and challenges of love, when you deal with your mortality.

Your culture will try to impose its pseudo-myth on you, its story of how things are and what is important. Your religion may try to impose its pseudo-myth, an escape from the world that is yours and from your precious identity. It will tell you it has a better way. But in the best of worlds, your culture and your religion help you find *your* myth, a narrative that will help your life unfold with intelligence, vision, and a strong sense of values. A myth is a living thing, and that is what Jesus offers: a narrative that gives life rather than an escape from life.

The First Secret: Imagination

Jesus describes this kingdom as a place where the familiar is turned upside down. It is like the mind shaken by a Zen master or inverted by a Sufi poet or turned inside out by a Christian mystic like Meister Eckhart, who said that the kingdom is in the human heart.[5] In Jesus' imagery, it requires being born spiritually or resurrecting after a life of sleep and death. Just as a fetus makes an entrance on the earthly scene at birth, so can anyone wake up in the kingdom by entering a newly imagined world. The idea of being reborn has been trivialized into an emotional, almost crazed embracing of a savior. But rebirth can be a powerful image for entering the world as if for the first time, where values and understanding are suddenly so radically different that you feel that you have been born again into life.

When I spoke of a secret in the Gospels, this is one thing I had in mind: seeing them as offering a new imagination or myth of human experience. As such, they could transform the world in which we live and offer a credible alternative to the self-destructive tendencies that dominate in the currently accepted myth.

If this sounds anticlimactic and not exactly radical, consider that your mythology is the very core of your beliefs, your understanding, and your values. It is the way you picture the world and interpret your experiences. Nothing is more basic or more crucial. Shifting from seeing life in the terms offered by a materialistic culture to the spiritual vision of Jesus is like exchanging one life for another and a tired old world for a fresh new one.

Jesus offers a set of values so radical, indeed, that few have taken it to his extremes. In his own life he showed what this new kind of existence would be like. The "good news"[6] is that you don't have to approach your life the way people have always done it: isolated and focused on yourself. Jesus tells you how to exit the realm of pure self-interest and absolute materialism—the current mythology—and enter an alternative way.

Some spiritual leaders present the Gospels as though they demand an expression of belief. If you say you believe that these texts describe the nature of things and other sacred texts do not, then you pass the test. But this approach is defensive, exclusive, and mental. An alternative is to value the Gospels for spelling out and inspiring a new way of life that is not defensive and self-centered. The rebirth may not be melodramatic.

For example, in recent years I have met many men and women who have told their stories of living the typical modern Western values—making good money, enjoying a prestigious job, and surrounding themselves with possessions that signify success. But in this humdrum life something happened. They came to the realization that their lives were not deeply satisfying, so they opted out. They found work that gave something to society. One man went from being a computer executive to teaching high school. A woman gave up a high-level job in a corporation to create a camp for girls. These life changes are entirely in the spirit of the Gospels and demonstrate how an ordinary person today "enters the kingdom."

The Kingdom of the Spiritual Imagination

My kingdom is not of this world.

—JOHN 18:36

When the Gospels mention the kingdom, they use two expressions: *basilea ouranou,* the kingdom of heaven or the sky, and *basilea theou,* the kingdom of God. *Ouranos* means sky or heaven, but it is also the name of the father god of the Greeks. We usually use the Latin form of his name, Uranus, well known in astrology. We could deepen our sense of the kingdom by reflecting on this deity, whose name echoes in the Gospel teaching about the kingdom.

In ancient Greek religion Ouranos was one of the primary realities, who, with his wife, Gaia, or Earth, brought forth all creatures. He is the creative father spirit imagined to exist in the fine ether of the sky, somewhat remote from earthly life yet very much involved in it. The cosmos began with these two realities, earth and sky, mother and father to all beings.

In the Greek language of the Gospels, using the word *Ouranos,* Jesus speaks of his father as "of the sky" and contrasts the father perspective with the earthly one. The kingdom of the father is a spiritual reality, not entirely worldly. Connecting with him, you raise your eyes to the sky and meet him on the mountain peak. As many commentators have noted, Jesus gives his central teachings, known as the Beatitudes, on a small mountain, an echo, perhaps, of the commandments given on Mount Sinai and a symbolic meeting place with the sky father.[7]

When you finally discover the kingdom, you live with a transcendent vision. You are in a heavenly kingdom, that is, a realm of meaning not limited to the unconscious assumptions of the average modern person, such as success, money, sexual dominance, and self-interest. You are in the world but not dominated by its unconscious values. Heaven is the spiritual dimension, the sphere of the father, a realm connected to daily life and yet beyond it.

When you find yourself in the kingdom, you will be in a different world, though at the factual level everything will be the same. The kingdom is translucent and empty. You don't see it in itself, but you see the world altered by it. Where one person sees competition and acts aggressively, you see community and act with compassion.

This change of heart, or *metanoia,* which we will discuss later in some detail, is, you might say, an archetypal event. It can happen in any person's life, as it did in Gandhi's youth, when through a series of indignities committed against him and his Indian compatriots in South Africa, he became a strong, vocal advocate for the poor and oppressed. Gandhi was certainly a citizen of the kingdom.

You see the same pattern in the story of the Buddha, who began life as a wealthy prince but was transformed at the sight of illness, poverty, and death. People wonder if Jesus ever studied with Buddhist teachers. I would not be at all surprised to learn that he did, and I have no doubt that Gautama Buddha was a citizen of the kingdom. The Gospels never say that you have to be Christian to enter the kingdom, but you do have to go through a profound shift in vision. The ancient tale of the Buddha's awakening is a story about metanoia.

Jesus, the Buddha, and Gandhi are examples of human beings electrified by the great vision of Ouranos and inspired to transform human life for the good. The Gospel story suggests that the Jesus way is like this: You are moved by a startling, new, iconoclastic vision for humanity. You live by principles contrary to those that lead only to self-destructiveness. You incarnate those values in your own life and urge them on your fellow humans.

The English poet William Blake wrote, "The Eternal Body of Man is The Imagination, that is, God himself, The Divine Body, Jesus: we are his members."[8] Blake's Jesus represents a particular way of imagining life. You read or hear what Jesus said and how he lived, and you see new possibilities. Regard for community radically replaces regard for self. Money remains an important part of life but is transformed by the spiritual vision of the kingdom. Sexuality has a central place, but it, too, is transformed by allowing spiritual values to color it. Jesus, in Blake's vision, is a powerful image of how life could be.

If you want to live the Jesus way, you do what he did: You live fully on this earth and become profoundly absorbed in secular life, but you also regularly consult the sky father. You look beyond the logic and values of earth and imagine a different order of things. You live in two dimensions: earth and sky, or as we usually say, heaven and earth.

Oscar Wilde said that Jesus' place is with the poets. Jesus was able to imagine himself carrying on his shoulders the fate of humanity and its healing. He was able to see every physical malady as a torment of the soul. He was able to give himself to the world as bread and wine and to take his vision so seriously as to die for it. He embodies an area yet to be explored with depth and seriousness: spiritual poetics and the role of the spiritual leader to open up worlds of meaning that are closed to pragmatic and literalistic eyes.

Reversal of Values

He summoned a child to stand before them and said,
"Unless you change and become like children, you won't
enter the kingdom of heaven. The person who is humble
like this child is greatest in the kingdom of heaven."

—MATTHEW 18:2–4

Jesus consistently describes the kingdom as a place where usual values are turned upside down. "The last shall be first." "Blessed are the poor." We have heard these statements many times and have probably understood them as pious platitudes about being humble and thinking well of the poor. But in context, these statements suggest living in a different world, where you don't make sense of your life just by making a good living and where you don't feel fulfilled by being more virtuous or more correct in your understanding of life than others. In the same way, Jesus presents a child as a prime example of what it means to be a citizen of the kingdom: an outsider, someone yet to be initiated into the conventions of society.

Talk about children risks sentimentalizing them and what they represent. And sentimentality around Jesus has been a problem, as seen in many prayers and depictions in art. Platitudes about Jesus abound, but the Gospels never sound sentimental. Even this passage in which Jesus says you have to be like a child is not sentimental.

A child's "beginner's mind," to use a phrase from Zen Buddhism, and emotional openness and lack of guile qualify you for the kingdom. In the kingdom, children don't become adults; adults become children. You lose the sophistication associated with conventional ideas and values. You start over, learning how to be a changed person in a new world.

One of my most tender memories as a father was the day my six-year-old daughter came to me with a thick telephone book and asked me to look up orphanages in our area. She wanted to visit one and make sure the children were safe and happy. This is a child's view of the world: innocent, compassionate, and free of the world-weariness and cynicism that corrode adult ideals. Of course, children are also self-absorbed and difficult, but they have a free pass to the kingdom because of their open hearts.

Here we also glimpse the subversive side of Jesus, evident in the threatening atmosphere around him as he advances his radical ideas. He warns that the principles you have always revered have to be abandoned. You may truly believe in working hard, making money, and raising children to be successful. You may judge people harshly who don't agree with your values. But Jesus teaches a life of service, simplicity of style, and an extraordinary degree of forgiveness. What he asks may seem unreasonable and impossible.

Jesus says that poverty is appropriate in the kingdom. The rich will be lucky if they can find their way into it. The person who has made a lot of mistakes will be welcomed. Whoever has been acting out sexually and changes his ways will be pardoned and feel a special welcome in this place. In a day when having money is a virtue and when sex offenders' names are listed in public places, these are challenging ideas, so confrontational that they are sometimes softened and interpreted to fit snugly into the status quo.

It's common for people to admit only those they consider virtuous into their "kingdom." For them, prisons, hospitals, and poor neighborhoods are foreign places and their inhabitants are strangers. In the Jesus kingdom, these people not only belong, they have a privileged position. That is why it is so contrary to the Gospel spirit to adapt the Jesus teachings to the cultural status quo. Jesus himself offers a radical alternative. His kingdom decidedly does not fit with the values of contemporary, conventional society.

Feeling like an outsider and standing out from the crowd because of your compassionate and forgiving values are signs that you may have found your way into the kingdom. Conversely, if you fit too snugly in the mass of humanity that has surrendered to narcissistic and paranoid values, you are not part of the father's kingdom. You have not yet found a way to blend, as Jesus did, a simple material life with a serious spiritual vision. You have not gone through the initiatory change of mind and heart, the metanoia, that Jesus clearly taught is necessary.

Recent history has revealed the violent response that the Jesus way may elicit: Mahatma Gandhi, Martin Luther King, Jr., John F. Kennedy, and Robert Kennedy shot down for their compassionate leadership; nuns raped, tortured, and killed for their community work. The new imagination that Jesus offers the world is not a set of platitudes; it is a challenge to live by compassionate, unconventional values.

The Gospels portray the kingdom as an imaginal world, having its own values and meanings that can transform human experience from one of hatred and aggression to one of love and community. The kingdom is not a place, not a thing, not an institution, not a membership. Maybe it is most like an attitude, a way of seeing, a turn of imagination that makes all the difference.

CHAPTER 2

A RADICAL SHIFT IN VISION

Metanoia

There was a man among the Pharisees, a Jewish leader, named Nicodemus. He came to Jesus at night and said, "We know you are a teacher who has come from God. No one could do the signs you do unless God were with him. In response Jesus said, "I have to tell you that no one could see the kingdom of God unless he were born from above." Nicodemus said to him, "How can someone who is old be born? Can you enter your mother's uterus and be born?" Jesus responded, "No one can enter the kingdom of God unless he is born from water and spirit."

—JOHN 3:1–5

This is a captivating scene. Late at night, Jesus and Nicodemus are discussing the very essence of the kingdom, and the Jewish leader is trying to understand. But he has a naïve idea about the meaning of rebirth. Jesus makes it clear to him that he is talking about rebirth in water, a washing away of the old way of life and a spiritual entry into a new life.

Nicodemus seems open and yet confused. He is in the midst of making sense of this new world of meaning. He is inching toward a radical shift in his way of thinking and living. He is going through the process of metanoia.

This change of mind is essential. It is deep-seated and revolutionary. On one side you live unconsciously, absorbing the worldview and values offered by your culture. On the other side, you think for yourself and experiment with the alternative reality Jesus embodies. If the shift in being isn't shocking, then it probably isn't in tune with the Gospel vision.

Meta-Noia

The word *metanoia* comes from two significant words: *meta* and *noia*. *Meta* means "after," sometimes "beyond." We use the word meta-morphosis for a worm becoming a butterfly. Just imagine the difference between these two beings. That is the *meta* of metanoia—a basic, unmistakable transformation. *Noia* is closely related to the word *Nous*, one that comes up frequently in philosophy and theology. It refers to the order of the universe, its logic and meaning. In the Neoplatonic philosophy of Plotinus, Nous is the second emanation to come into being. In other words, it is the basic building block of the world of meaning you inhabit.

In ordinary usage, *meta* means "change" and *noia* means "mind," and so metanoia can mean to change your mind. But with the rich history of the word in the background, you can catch a glimpse of how radical a change it implies. You don't just change your mind; you go from worm to butterfly. You go through a radical metamorphosis and your very being is transformed. You live in a different world.

For centuries people have had the habit of viewing the Gospels in moralistic terms. They tend to think: *How do I know what is good and what is bad? How can I be on the side of good? How can I avoid punishment for my bad behavior?*

In this atmosphere, the word *metanoia* has been translated routinely as "repentance," a term having to do with moral feeling. But if you were to go through the Gospels and retranslate this one word, in its various forms, as "shift in vision" or "discovery of a new world of meaning," you would have an altogether different take on these ancient writings. Your task would be to live a different life, not just feel bad about the mistakes you have made and live in fear of punishment. And this reading would be true to the text and more in tune with the spirit of the Gospels.

Metanoia is the process by which you enter the kingdom. Jesus asks for a deep shift in worldview. He requires a change in the myth by which we live. He asks for such a profound change that a sincere, thoughtful man like Nicodemus can hardly make sense of it.

In my own life, the most troubling change in life vision came to me as I was leaving a religious order and deciding not to become a priest, a goal that had been strong and tenacious in me for 13 or 14 years. I had seen many colleagues come and go and assumed from my own feelings that I would be constant.

The change wasn't immediate, though it was final and clear. I had been living in the protected atmosphere of a monastery, or priory; then I went to the university in the city and developed warm friendships there. I began to see my life in a larger context and came to accept that my destiny was there. I would disappoint many people with my decision and many would never understand it. But it was a Gospel choice: do I live the sheltered life of a monk and priest, or do I risk a move out into the world? I chose the latter, and the process was one of metanoia. Paradoxically, I believe that had I remained on the track for priesthood I would not have entered the kingdom. I would have chosen the self-protective way rather than the way of compassion.

One of the most difficult things to do is to change the way you imagine your place in life. Nothing is more challenging. On the other hand, once this change takes place, nothing could be more vitalizing. Truly, it's as if you are born a second time. Your eyes open to a different world. You go back into the waters of the womb and emerge in a higher reality. The Greek word can mean either "born again" or "born above." I prefer to hear both meanings at the same time.

If you don't go through this deep change of heart and mind, you aren't in the kingdom. It's as simple as that. You can believe anything you want. You can go to church as often as you want. You can be virtuous and noble. But if you don't escape from default reality and enter a new level of existence—if you aren't baptized, in an existential sense, not just a formal ritual—then you are outside the kingdom. You have missed the central theme of the Gospels.

Should you experience a transformation in the way you imagine the whole of your existence, you will feel awake. Jesus and the Buddha, who was known as the Awakened One, are after the same goal. They remind us that our usual ways of thinking are outmoded, indeed deathly. Before, in your daily unconscious life, in the cycle of everyday existence Buddhists call *samsara*—outside the kingdom—you have been asleep. But now, through a profound shift in vision, you wake up.

Metanoia as Zen Satori

"The time has been completed," he said.
"The kingdom of God is close. Shift your vision,
and put your trust in the exciting new ideas."

—MARK 1:15

Like the kingdom itself, metanoia is not terribly visible. You don't have to go off to a cave or the desert in pursuit of it, though some have done so, and you don't have to engage in extreme techniques of meditation and contemplation, though, again, some have gone this route. You may be in the thick of family life, doing your work and getting along. But suddenly you realize that all the self-serving assumptions around you are inadequate and dehumanizing. If they were all turned inside out, the world would be a better place. This realization suddenly and intuitively puts you in the kingdom.

There are some images in Jesus' story that would connect metanoia with the Zen experience of *satori*, a sudden awakening, or, in the surprisingly apt words of Zen scholar D. T. Suzuki, "the unfolding of a new world."[9] It is also similar to the inverted logic portrayed in Sufi stories. In one such story, which is not unlike a parable

Jesus might tell, a man gets lost and consumes all the food he has with him. Then he spots a bulging bag lying on the ground and hopes it is full of food. He is sad to find it filled with pearls.

This kind of reversal of values is much in the spirit of Jesus. It is more important to be solidly nourished than to be rich in possessions. He tells story after story to show how life could be transformed if we simply reconsidered our basic assumptions. What is more important when you're starving: food or jewelry? In the spiritual sphere, what is more important: money or vision? Notice once again, by the way, the key image of the pearl.

I don't want to give the impression that metanoia is a sudden, shocking emotional revelation, like Saint Paul being thrown from his horse. In one sense it's a microscopic shift from one way of seeing the world to another. On one side of it you interpret your world according to conventional values, and on the other side you suddenly understand things differently. The realization may come after years of study and searching or in a moment's realization. The change may go unnoticed at first, until one day you realize you are living a different life.

Metanoia is one of four Greek terms that sum up the Jesus way. The others are *basilea, agape,* and *therapeia*— the kingdom, the law of love, and the work of healing. All four are implicated in each other, all four going on at once, all four defining each other.

Change of heart
brings you into the kingdom
where you discover the power of love
to heal.

Here are the fundamentals of the Jesus philosophy. You change profoundly: You don't just repent and feel sorry for your mistakes. You adopt an utterly unconventional point of view. You live in a different reality, even though you are still working out your worldly life. Two streams now define your life: earthly concerns and a spiritual vision. This change leads to a life based on love, a love rooted in radical and profound respect for the other. Eventually you realize that your chief role in life is to heal. That is how Jesus lived and that is what the Gospels teach.

The Alchemy of Baptism

[John the Baptist said,] "I baptize you in water for a shift in vision [metanoia]. But after me, someone is coming who is more powerful than I and whose shoes I am not worthy to carry. He will baptize you in holy spirit and fire."

—Matthew 3:11

Baptism is the symbolic and ritual expression of metanoia, and this passage reveals that there are two aspects to baptism, symbolized in water and fire. Water dissolves the old world and is an image of death, cleansing, solution, and the amniotic fluid from which you are born. Fire, a slightly different form of change, burns away the old life and incites you to live a new one.

Jesus stands in the water of the Jordan River to be baptized by John, and the sky opens up, showing shamanically how the otherworld is made accessible through this aquatic ritual. Later, at Pentecost, the students are gathered together and a vision of tongues of fire appears and they understand this to be an image of spirit—the next step in the rite of passage. In the first, water, they enter a new reality. In the second, fire, they are thoroughly transformed, their old ways burned away, so they can now act on behalf of the new reality.[10] In baptism by water they are born to a new understanding and a new life. In baptism by fire they are completely purged of old ideas and values and made ready for the work of teaching and healing.

The fiery catharsis transforms you so deeply that you acquire the power to heal. This is a great mystery, attested by many shamans and yogis: before you can be a real healer, your egotism has to be burned away. Your neurotic agendas, so long in the way, must vanish so you can be a conduit of healing. Followers of Jesus often take a rational and moral approach to the teachings, which then seem far distant from those of shamans and yogis. But what if that breach were healed and the Gospels became a source of intelligent, grounded, yet mystical healing? Then we would see clearly that metanoia is a change in being, not just mind and behavior. When you undergo this transformation, radically and profoundly, you become a healing presence.

Baptism in water shows poetically what happens in the soul when a person's vision shifts out of the conventional into the spiritual. First, there is the sensation of death and rebirth, a being born into a new and different world. Secondly, there is the cleansing of former difficult and destructive patterns. Thirdly, there is an opening to the spiritual, a conduit to the father spirit and source of life. There, you are connected to your absolute roots and depth, and how you imagine life and live it is in accord with your nature and the nature of the world.

Jesus' baptism set him up for his crucifixion. But Jesus was at home not only in water but also in fire. You don't find much about fire in the canonical Gospels, but in the Gospel of the Savior (107:12), an early noncanonical Gospel, Jesus uses this image about himself and his work:

If one is [near] to me, he will [burn.] I am the [fire] [that] blazes; who [is near] [to me, is] near to [the fire]; who is far from me, is far from life.[11]

The Gospel of Philip makes a related comment:

The soul and the spirit are born of water and of fire.[12]

As always with mention of the elements in spiritual literature, we have to understand them both as they are in nature and as they signify deeper psychological and spiritual realities. There is something cool and liquid about the soul, hot and flame-like about the spirit. Jesus embodies both of these basic qualities, as we do, and the notion of metanoia involves both: Deep in our souls we have to change in order to enter the kingdom, and in the far reaches of our ideals and vision we have to transcend the conventional and know something about spiritual matters. We have to be reborn in water and tempered in fire.

A clear example is Martin Luther King, Jr., spending years studying theology, completing his baptism of water, and then facing a hostile world that failed to appreciate his vision. In his public life the fire in him was necessary and helped him complete his mission.

Like Jesus, he confessed to feeling fear for his life, and, like Jesus, he spoke his challenging words with strength and passion.

> *So, make fruit appropriate for the new shift in vision*
> *[metanoia].*
>
> —MATTHEW 3:8

"Fruit" here means follow-through, doing something as a result of your change of heart. Jesus sends his students into the world to establish the change of heart that would also change the world. Establishing the kingdom in the world doesn't mean converting people to a belief system but creating the climate in which a spiritual vision combines with deep engagement with life. The result is a different world order, where paranoia and its consequent aggression are replaced with neighborly respect and a sense of community. Metanoia is the necessary shift in feeling and understanding that allows the new world order to come into existence.

Without metanoia, without a real change in understanding, we apply old solutions to our problems and get nowhere. A deep-seated shift in vision leads to fresh solutions. Recent history offers examples of this kind of shift: Gandhi, Martin Luther King, Jr., Mother Teresa, and Nelson Mandela, for example. From the past we have the example of the Buddha, Lao-tzu, Mohammed, Saint Francis, Hildegard of Bingen, and, in her small way, Emily Dickinson. Each reimagined the world and lived accordingly, using his and her specific talents for healing. Each was known as a radical visionary and healer.

Anyone who wants to follow the Jesus way and be part of the kingdom has to do the same: cultivate a fresh new vision about human life and then do what is possible to heal the world.

Metanoia comes at a great cost. You are asked to give up an understanding of life that has been in place for a long time. You are invited to live by a set of values that don't offer ego rewards at first but only reward you after you discover the joy of community and agape, the law of love. You are also faced with the challenge of living by values that contradict those of normal society. The new world you find on the other side of change demands courage—and sometimes your very life.

CHAPTER 3

WATER TO WINE

Jesus the Epicurean

On the third day there was a wedding at Cana in Galilee, and Jesus' mother was there. Jesus and his students had also been invited to the wedding. When the wine had run out, Jesus' mother said to him, "There's no more wine."

Jesus said, "What does that have to do with us? My hour isn't here yet."

His mother told the waiters, "Do whatever he says."

There were six stone water jars standing there, used by the Jews for rites of purification. Each held twenty to thirty gallons. Jesus said to them, "Fill the jars with water," and they filled them to the brim.

Jesus said, "Pour some out and give it to the wedding planner."

*They did so, and the wedding planner tasted the water that
had become wine. He didn't understand where it had come
from, though the waiters who had poured the water knew.*

*The wedding planner called for the groom and said,
"People bring out the good wine first and then, after
the guests have been drinking, get the cheap stuff.
But you kept the good wine until now."*

*This was the first of the signs Jesus made at Cana in
Galilee. He revealed his glory, and his students trusted him.*

—JOHN 2:1–11

This story is often referred to as the first of Jesus'
miracles, but Cana is more than a miracle; its resonant,
ancient images convey the very essence of Jesus' message
to humankind: look at the world anew and find heaven
on earth.

At one level, this is a parable about marriage, and as
such it offers rich insight into the deep significance of
matrimony, an important ingredient in deep community.
At another level, it uses marriage as a metaphor for the
shift in consciousness that is the essence of Jesus' teaching. The story of Cana is not just a chronicle of the first of
many miracles; it is a parable describing the very heart of
Jesus' teaching, and it prefigures the events to come: the
teachings, the community, and the crucifixion.

A Gospel of Pleasure

This is an unusual miracle story in that Jesus is in
the company of his mother, and she plays a pivotal

role. His mother's concern for the family moves him—a strong sign of his soulfulness. She pays no attention to his refusal, and in a flash—there is not a beat between his orders to the waiters to fill the jars and his suggestion that they give a taste to the maitre d'—by a mysterious alchemy plain water transmutes into exquisite wine.

The sheer humanity in this story is part of its message: Jesus responds to his mother's concern and offers a first glance at his teaching during a party, over something as ordinary as wine running out. At the same time, the wedding party represents the current human condition: our wine—our vitality, complexity, and spirit—is running out.

The change of water to wine signifies a much deeper kind of change in the human spirit—from plain unconsciousness to an intoxicating vision. It is the central theme of the Gospels: go through a change of vision and discover life in all its abundance and intensity.

Wine is a symbol for the deep pleasures of life. As a more complex image—grapes crushed and then fermented to make a liquid that can affect consciousness—it points to a defining quality of Jesus' person and his teaching. The transformation from unconscious, self-absorbed living to a way of life shaped by love of self and others is miraculous. It is as striking as the imperceptible shift from water to wine. The miracle signifies metanoia.

In the context of a wedding party and over the issue of wine, Jesus also shows his epicurean side. Epicurus is a much misunderstood philosopher who taught that simple pleasure is the foundation of a good life. Contrary to popular understanding, he spoke against hedonism, or extreme pleasure for its own sake. He especially honored friendship, good vegetarian food, conversation, gatherings of men and women students together, and joyful community.

Jesus has much in common with Epicurus, as we'll see in a later chapter. The Gospels are full of scenes where he is eating, cooking, serving food, arranging dinner, caring for his students, and enjoying the company of people at table.[13] Especially in the noncanonical Gospels, he laughs with his friends over their extreme urgency to find answers to unanswerable questions and is quick to forgive and offer comfort.

The simple shift from a punitive conception of Jesus and his work to an Epicurean appreciation of human pleasure would transform the thrust of his teaching. Epicureanism, a deep acceptance of the human need for freedom from pain and anxiety, is a cure for much of the depression, meanness, and repression that so often afflicts religious and spiritual people. Jesus offers healing of soul through his kind and openhearted embrace of the human condition. Imagine what Christianity would be like if it were as Epicurean in style as Jesus was.

The Dionysian

Another major Greek theme that deepens and com-plexifies Jesus' Epicureanism lies hidden in the story of Cana—the mystery of Dionysus. The Greeks honored a child god whose body was torn to pieces and who was accessible to his followers in wine. Dionysus embodies the reconciliation of extreme opposites—life and death, male and female, spirituality and sensuality. The scene in Euripides' *Bakkai*, our major source of knowledge about the Dionysian, where Dionysus stands before King

Pentheus as the king tries to chain and imprison him is stunningly close to the image of Jesus interrogated by the Roman official Pontius Pilate. It is the same confrontation between rigid might and order on one side and supple warmth and simple humanity on the other.

It's curious that just 18 miles from Nazareth, where Jesus grew up, there was a major temple to the god Dionysus.[14] This god, a scandal to many, represented a full engagement with life, so given to risk that through the spirit of Dionysus in your life you experience the "death" of failing, being misunderstood, and being torn apart by conflicting passions.

The Dionysian and the Epicurean approaches to life—affirming, subtle, and positive about pleasure and vitality—are essential aspects of Jesus' teaching. Both appear just beneath the surface of the Cana story—yet another reason why this narrative is central to establishing the nature of the kingdom.[15]

To be a student of Jesus is to pursue the pleasures that foster human warmth and community. Anyone familiar with monasticism knows that monks, while austere and spiritually focused, apparently understand this lesson. Though ascetic and contemplative, they cultivate the simple pleasures of food and culture. A recent book on the life and times of Michelangelo describes a community of monks in his time that had an exquisite garden and great paintings. The monks distilled perfumes, prepared medicines, manufactured stained-glass windows, and concocted pigments for artists.[16] The bread, wine, crafts, and architectural splendor of the monasteries are not incidental to the life but expressive of its core genius and its central spirituality.

I myself lived as a Catholic monk for 13 years and know well the Dionysian and Epicurean aspects of that life. I enjoyed many simple pleasures of the common life as well as difficult conflicts over love and meaning, solitude and community, and celibacy and sexuality. Jesus is the prototype of giving oneself to life, especially the Dionysian and Epicurean pleasures of beauty, sensuality, and intoxication.

The Wine-Dark Mystery

While simple pleasure is the *prima facie* content of Cana, the scene quickly deepens as you reflect on the specific images. You can see, for instance, the foretelling of another crucial gathering of friends and students at the supper Jesus arranged and presided over shortly before his death, where he said that the wine they were all drinking was his very blood. There is a significant arc to the story of his life, a movement from the wine of Cana to the wine of the "last supper." History focuses on the latter, but it would also be good to remember Cana. The full mystery of Jesus' teaching is incomplete without it.

If Cana is the first miracle, maybe we should consider this the first lesson in Jesus spirituality: Be human, understand the importance of play and simple sensual pleasures, and listen to your family. Then go deeper. See Cana as a foretaste of the supper at which wine will signify the lifeblood at risk when you offer your life-affirming philosophy to a cruel world.

To live this intriguing way of the Dionysian Jesus is to say yes to life every step of the way, in spite of the possibility that you will be torn apart, judged, and crucified. You live and die in each moment. You love so much that you risk separation and loss. You are so creative and original that you shock your friends and neighbors and are lacerated with criticism. You are so loving and so powerful that no one can stuff you into any notion of conventional gender, and, like Jesus, you may be full of contradictory qualities: soft and bold, powerful and tender, radical and simple.

Thomas Merton, the monk, wished for a little sensual affection and an occasional drink of alcohol within the austere life of his Trappist community. He had the Cana spirit: he was both an ascetic and an Epicurean, just like Jesus. In the thick of his love for a nurse he had met, he referred to the experience as a "great trauma" that had "broken in" on him—echoes of Dionysus.[17]

Jesus not only told his students to drink wine as a reminder of his blood, but he also said, "I am the vine; you are the branches." Jesus is not only the grape that is crushed or crucified; he is also the grapevine, the origin of the wine mystery. In an ancient vase painting, Dionysus appears in a boat surrounded by grape vines. Jesus could be sitting next to him. Even if you don't literally drink wine, you can learn the intoxicating effect of giving yourself to the pleasures of nature and of human community. After all, it is this invisible wine that is the ultimate mystery of the Jesus way. Wine is the symbol or sacrament; being fermented and intoxicated is the experience.

Sufi poets often talk about their union with God as intoxication in a similar way. A highly regarded poet from the 7th century, Farriduddin Attar, writes about divine love:

Eternal Wisdom made all things in love,
By love are all bewildered, stupefied,
Intoxicated by the wine of love.[18]

Thomas Aquinas, too, talks about intoxication in a theological sense: "Wine," he notes in his commentary on Boetius's *De Trinitate*, "often signifies divine wisdom," whereas "water signifies secular wisdom."[19] This is Cana symbolism: water becoming wine.

It is not the essence of Jesus to be inhibited, controlled, righteous, and fearful. On the contrary, Jesus gives himself to life. Wine is his blood, the flowing substance that gives him his vitality. Imagine if wine were flowing through your veins, not just making you plain drunk but sending you into paroxysms of joy and abandon. That is the Dionysian will to live, and that is a significant side of Jesus. To be his student is to risk the explosive joy as well as the annihilating suffering of a human being who gives himself to life.[20]

My own experience of Christianity, so rich and positive in many ways, has also been depressive, weighted down with authority, demands of purity, and the suppression of individual creativity. It was only after studying the Greeks, whose idea of divinity embraces sexuality, sensuality, and the joys of life, that I could see the potential for a more Dionysian reading of the Gospels. I learned from C. G. Jung, my teacher David Miller, and others that Cana is an essential stop on the journey through the Gospels.

The Alchemy of a Wedding

The story of Cana also has something to say about human relationships and about marriage in particular. It's no accident that Jesus began his life work at a wedding. Marriage is yet another reversal of expectations.

Ordinarily, in spiritual matters, the focus is on the individual and his or her striving for understanding and moral perfection. But Jesus demonstrates that in the kingdom, marriage is one of the prime settings in which the transformation from plain living to new vision can take place—water to wine.

Two people who have lived their separate lives decide to share those lives. Everyone knows the process is difficult, like crushing grapes to get the juice. But over time those raw and untested lives take on new complexity and richness, due to the sharing and the struggle. Like grape juice turning into wine, the lives ferment in an alchemy that transmutes the two from people trying to get along individually to a couple discovering the deep mystery of a shared life.

At Cana, water is the image for simple survival as a single person, while wine symbolizes the more complex state of marriage. Single people have their own struggles and different ways to ripen and become interesting, but married couples have a built-in method of development. Just learning how to get along and make a life out of their union is a miracle.

Marriage is a spiritual act because it requires constant transcending of selfishness, a conscious decision to live a good life, and a generous spilling over of those lessons in raising children and dealing with family and neighbors. A real marriage has its own inherent spirituality and is quite fittingly symbolized as water becoming wine. It is entirely appropriate that a marriage take place in a church or temple, and it wouldn't be a bad idea to read the story of Cana in that ritual, to be reminded of the many ways in which marriage is both a miracle and a spiritual state.

Today, many argue about whether Jesus was married or celibate, whether he had a lover and children, and whether he embodies sexual abstinence or a special kind of eroticism. However you resolve these issues for yourself, there is no denying his sensitive participation at the wedding in Cana. With his stunning manifestation of compassionate power he blesses marriage. He suggests that the spiritual revolution he came to announce can be seen in so simple a thing as a wedding.

Jesus' respect for marriage, making it the very first occasion for the manifestation of the kingdom, indicates that what takes place in marriage is of the essence of the kingdom. People come together and share their individualities. They spend a lifetime together, growing as people and as a couple. They may have children and grandchildren as their love transforms their world. And all of this is a model of the kingdom.

People everywhere can come together in this model of marriage. They keep their individuality but share a life. They become more and more complex as a community, as the blend of individuality and togetherness intensifies over time. The union proves to be a highly creative development in the lives of the individuals and in their families and communities. Cana is a microcosm of the kingdom, while it also symbolizes the nature of the kingdom. In other words, water to wine signifies the dynamics of marriage, and marriage signifies the dynamic of the kingdom as a whole.

The Transformed Life

Notice that the water Jesus turns into wine is special water reserved for rites of purification. Jesus shifts the spiritual ideal from purifying water to intoxicating vitality. With him we move from moralism to joy, from repressive rules to the enjoyment of life's deep pleasures.

Moralism, with its companion feelings of guilt, is an aspect of life lived unconsciously, without intelligent reflection. As such, it is the way of the world and is generally more widespread than the thoughtful life. This unconsciousness is evident in worldwide conflicts and in domestic violence and child abuse. The shift in awareness represented by Cana could transform this sad condition and usher in new levels of joy and satisfaction.

That Jesus was an Epicurean contrasts with the tendency of some of his later followers to be only ascetic or puritan, denying the value of pleasure and desire. Indeed, the above description of what it means to walk in the shoes of this Jesus could transform the way people understand every word of the Gospels. But the matter goes even deeper.

The tale of the wedding at Cana is not only the first sign of Jesus' life as a teacher and healer, it is the cornerstone and key of the entire enterprise. The image of water of purification transformed into wine tells the entire story of Jesus' mission. Our tendency toward being virtuous and pure, especially for those of us raised in religious families, is changed radically in the life and teachings of Jesus. Instead of striving for purity and innocence, we aim for vitality and pleasure, a life of joyous intimacy with friends, family, and neighbors. Instead of living under obligation and defining ourselves by hard work, we could appreciate the importance of pleasure. We could see that the flat ordinary life is like plain water, while the spiritually alive life in real community is more like wine.

You might object that the real mystery and core of the teaching is the death and resurrection of Jesus. But the story of Cana is a poetic version of that pattern: the grape crushed and the water "resurrected" as wine. Both Jesus and Dionysus were torn apart in a savage execution, and both "rise" again, just as the crushed grape rises as wine. The parallel is an ancient one.

I look back at photographs from my wedding in 1992. Who is that thin guy with the dark hair? And who is that woman so full of life and promise? I think of that moment in time as one of sheer joy, with friends and family around who were part of the story that brought that love to fruition. I remember the wine we drank at the small party afterward, a Louis Latour Pouilly-Fuissé. Nowadays I will buy a bottle occasionally for remembrance. Why the wine? Why the party? Because they symbolize and ritualize the transformation that took place that day when we entered the kingdom in a special way and began to craft a life of the kind the Gospel espouses.

My wife pursues an intense Sikh form of spirituality, and I continue to be a "Zen Catholic" whose spirituality is so baked into life that it is nearly invisible. This odd coupling, revealed in children who are very spiritual, creative, and individual, is, as I see it, deep within the philosophy of the Gospels. It is Cana all over again.

CHAPTER 4

LOVE IN THE KINGDOM

Agape

Jesus loved [egapa] Martha and her sister and Lazarus.

—JOHN 11:5

If you were to read the Gospels in Greek, you would find the word *agape* used again and again to describe the love that defines the kingdom. In ancient Greece, agape referred to the value placed on jewels and other precious objects. This nuance fits the Gospels, where Jesus places high value on people who are normally rejected. He sees through surface problems of illness, weakness, and failure to the jewel at the core of the person.

Agape is an alternative to hatred, suspicion, judgment, and paranoia. It is less an emotion and more an orientation toward life. You face the world with an open heart rather than with a suspicious or punitive one. You don't reject and distance the world from you but rather embrace it. In the kingdom you reach out precisely toward those who in ordinary reality are ostracized.

In English the word *love* sounds sentimental. If you think of love primarily as an emotion, you may work yourself up to feel something for other people without changing the way you live. But the agape of the Gospels is not just a feeling; it's a stance, a position, an evaluation that generates respect.

The parable of the prodigal son is a perfect example.

A man had two sons. The younger spoke to his father, "Father, give me my share of the property coming to me." So he divided the money between the sons. A few days later, the younger son put together everything he had and went off to another country where he wasted his money away.

After he had spent everything, the country suffered a famine and he began to need things. So he got a job with someone who lived in that country and he was sent out into the fields to feed the pigs. He wanted to fill his own belly with the stalks he was feeding the pigs, but no one gave him anything.

But then he came to himself and said, how many of my father's workers have more than enough bread, and I am here starving. I will get going and return to my father and tell him, "Father, I have failed both you and heaven. I am not worthy any longer to be known as your son. Let me be one of your workers." So he got up and went to his father.

He was still far off when his father saw him and was filled with compassion. He ran and put his arms around his son and kissed him again and again. The son said to him, "Father, I have failed you and heaven. I'm not worthy any longer to be known as your son."

His father said to the servants. "Hurry. Get the best robe for him, and sandals, and put a ring on his finger. Get the mature calf and butcher it. We'll eat and celebrate. For my son was dead, but now he has come back to life. He was lost, but now he is found." Then they began to celebrate.

During this time the older son was out in the field. When he came close to the house, he heard music and dancing. He called to one of the servants and asked what it was all about. "Your brother has arrived," he said, "and your father has killed a mature calf because he has his son back in good condition."

He was angry and wouldn't go in, so his father went out and begged him. But he answered his father, "Listen! All these years I have served you and never went against your orders, and you never gave me even a young goat so I could have a party with my friends. But when your son returns, the one who wasted your bounty with prostitutes, you butcher the mature calf for him."

The father said to him, "Son, you are always with me, and everything I have is yours. But we had to have a party and be happy, because your brother was dead and has come back to life. He was lost and has been found."

—LUKE 15:11–32

Like all the parables, this one shows what it is like to live in the kingdom. It contains two themes, common to other stories and teachings, that are compelling and confusing.

First, the reversal. Although the father loves his solid son who has remained with him and been trustworthy, he also loves the son who has squandered all his money and lived a wasted life. It is the rule of the kingdom to go out of the way to receive and accept someone who has failed miserably, even morally.

Second, the resurrection. Jesus told his students to bring the dead to life. We have a tendency to think literally and imagine an unnatural miracle of a Frankensteinian sort. But this story assures us that Jesus is talking about restoring a dead soul and spirit. The prodigal son was dead to family, virtue, and sense. But now he comes back to life and wants to change his ways. Resurrection is metanoia.[21]

The prodigal son has a change of heart. He acknowledges that he has failed (traditionally translated as "sinned"), and owning up to failure in this way, Jesus often says, is part of the conversion experience—conversion not in the sense of becoming a follower but going through a radical, life-transforming change of vision. Jesus doesn't applaud a squandered life, but he places high value on a person who has made mistakes and then had a change of heart. Metanoia is of great importance in his vision, and it is always a return to love. You risk life, make a mistake, and return with new conviction. It is not merely a change of mind but a change of heart as well.

Most of us know the experience of wasting time, talents, money, and other resources; of making mistakes and bad judgments; of associating with the wrong people and not always being able to be sexually virtuous. In Jesus' eye, these failures in judgment are precious in a certain way. They can be redeemed and perhaps transformed into a meaningful life that may be better, in the long run, than that of the person who lives virtuously from the beginning.

Naïve virtue is often a defense against life's complexity. It can be an unwillingness to take risks and discover what life is all about. After making some mistakes, you are ready for another, more sophisticated kind of virtue. Then you enter the kingdom with your eyes open, as an adult. Your sense of virtue is tougher and darker. This second kind of virtue seems rare among religious people and is not often discussed. Religion usually champions primary, naïve, unbroken virtuousness, but that is not the way of the Gospels.

A by-product of metanoia, of having lived a full life, taken risks, and made mistakes, is empathy for those who have done similarly. You are capable of forgiveness, another key action that Jesus demonstrates again and again. Forgiveness is not easy, nor is it cheap. It arises when you feel sufficient empathy with the human condition that your own excessive feelings of virtue don't get in the way.

The compassionate father in the story, who surely mirrors the father Jesus speaks of as his heavenly authority, loves both sons, both kinds of people, but has special regard for the one who fails and then restores himself. From a "heavenly" or high spiritual point of view, making mistakes out of some deep ignorance or interior misalignment and then reconsidering your entire life has great value.

Thomas Merton, who lived a Bohemian lifestyle in New York before becoming a strict Cistercian monk, was well aware of the gap between spiritual rebirth and the old conventional persona. As a monk he took the name Father Louis. In his powerful autobiography, *The Seven Storey Mountain,* he says:

> There was this shadow, this double, this writer who had followed me into the cloister.
>
> He is still on my track. He rides my shoulders, sometimes, like the old man of the sea. I cannot lose him. He still wears the name of Thomas Merton. Is it the name of an enemy?
>
> He is supposed to be dead.
>
> But he stands and meets me in the doorway of all my prayers, and follows me into church. He kneels with me behind the pillar, the Judas, and talks to me all the time in my ear.[22]

The shadow of a wasted life doesn't disappear after metanoia, but remains as a catalyst keeping your thoughts sharp and your intentions suitably complex. If Merton was an enemy to Father Louis, he was also beloved.

Don't we all have a Judas, someone who would betray and spoil our virtue, whispering in our ear at the very moment we're trying to follow our ideals? This shadow angel, the antipode and maybe antidote to the noble guardian angel, keeps us honest and complex. We need that shadow to be in the kingdom, because Jesus insisted that those who made grave mistakes belonged in his community of followers.

Jesus is not a purist or perfectionist. He appreciates the mysterious complexity of human life and therefore is patient with human foibles. Both Thomas Merton and

Father Louis lived first in the monastery and then in a hermitage, the one shadow to the other. Jesus favors this kind of complexity and is impatient with unadulterated purity.

You shall love [agapeseis] the Lord your God with your whole heart, your whole soul, and your whole intention. This is the greatest and first instruction. The second is similar: You shall love [agapeseis] your neighbor as yourself.

—Matthew 22:37–39

In this summary statement about how to live in the kingdom, Jesus once again addresses the two streams: spirit and soul. You have to love the source of life on one side and your neighbor and your world on the other. One is implicated in the other. By holding precious the vision of life you find in your spirituality, you can learn to love that which is nearest and closest to you. And, vice versa, you can be engaged with the exalted spirit only when you show love for the mundane world around you.

This is a difficult lesson, for the temptation in all spiritual matters is to split spirit and world. High in your spiritual absorption, you may fail to see the importance of everyday life with its puny concerns and difficult relationships and annoying people. You may find your sexuality a problem and assign it accordingly to the rubbish heap of human passion. You may not see how your spirituality is worked out through your ordinary, humble affairs of life. But Jesus says, as clearly as can be stated, that love of God, love of neighbor, and love of self all go together.

If you probe deep enough into this important question of love, you see that you can't love another person unless you love yourself. (I might prefer to say "love your soul," because this is not a selfish love that we're talking about.) It also works in the other direction: you can't love yourself unless you have the openness to love another. These two are inseparable, and if it seems to you that you are doing one and not the other, you are probably weak in both.

I'm giving you a new commandment, that you love [agapate] each other. As I have loved [agapesa] you, you love each other. In this everyone will know that you are students of mine: that you have love [agapen] for each other.

—JOHN 13:34–35

It's curious that with this statement being so clear and unequivocal, using the word *agape* three times in a short space, Christians still honor the Ten Commandments of the old law as the standard of moral behavior. Jesus here offers a new basis for morality, not just a new set of rules. The old law, with its minimal and negative requirements, is replaced with a new kind of law, an inspiring vision rooted in love rather than obligations based in anxiety. As I keep saying, Jesus is not uttering moral platitudes but rather suggesting a new philosophy. He is not adding to the Ten Commandments; he is replacing them.

Obeying rules is an entirely different motivation and philosophy of life. The danger in it is to become legalistic, find too many loopholes, lose the spirit of ethical living, and ignore issues of justice and morality not immediately apparent in the mere outline of commandments. On the other hand, the danger in a morality of love is to sentimentalize the notion of love, restrict the phrase "love each other" to mean a select group, and overlook the radical nature of the command.

Agape is not the desire to possess or to have gratification. Its first meaning is "to show affection." Secondarily, as we saw, it can also mean "to treat as precious." Jesus' way is a philosophy of affection, a matter of heart and soul. It is not an abstract love, as merely wanting the best for humankind or striving toward an ideal. Jesus' example shows that agape is genuine acceptance of those who are rejected and judged, a warm embrace of a variety of people, and consistent attention to close friends.

Abraham Lincoln demonstrated this rule of agape in his determination to end slavery and not to engage in preemptive war. Referring to the fame of his political rival Stephen Douglas, he said:

> "I affect no contempt for the high eminence he has reached. So reached, that the oppressed of my species, might have shared with me in the elevation, I would rather stand on that eminence, than wear the richest crown that ever pressed a monarch's brow."[23]

This sentiment and orientation, to deliver the species from oppression, describes agape as presented in the Gospels more accurately than the usual platitudes about loving your neighbor. If everyone felt and thought this way, we would be living in a radically different world, the kingdom of heaven.

On the other hand, the attitude conveyed in Lincoln's words may be buttressed by an unusual degree of feeling toward others. By all accounts Jesus was an affectionate person. He held children to him, he held hands in dance, he dined with friends and strangers, he felt his friendships deeply, and he dealt with his students warmly, often laughing at their sincere efforts to understand him. This image of him comes through clearly in both the canonical and noncanonical Gospels.

He models a personality that is accepting of human frailty, rarely judgmental, capable of deep friendship, and generally a healing presence. Today, it would seem more important for his student to emulate these qualities than to get the teaching exactly right and follow all the rules.

Established approaches to the Gospels usually place rules and authority at the base of the teachings and then urge sentimental love within that context. The Gospels are clear in suggesting the opposite: Love is unsentimental, and it is the base. Out of it arises a different notion of commandment, more an understanding of life that naturally gives rise to agape.

All the while, we have to keep in mind that Jesus is talking about a new kind of earth, about spiritual values that could transform the way human beings live. He is not simply telling you how to live a virtuous life. He speaks parables, not platitudes. He is envisioning heaven on earth.

Heaven here is not utopian. Heaven is a condition in which you live an ordinary life fully and uninhibitedly based on the idea of respect, on what Albert Schweitzer called "reverence for life." Heaven is not some impossible, idealized world; it is ordinary life made brilliant by a philosophy of mutual respect.

*Whoever has my instructions and follows them is the one
who loves [agapon] me. The one who loves [agapon] me
will be loved [agapethesetai] by my father, and I will love
[agapeso] him and will make myself visible to him.*

—JOHN 14:21

This entire passage is saturated with the word *agape*
and suggests that observing this law of love means that
you will be loved absolutely by the very source of life.
Life itself will love you if you live by the rule of love.

Again, we have to find a way to imagine this recip-
rocal kind of love, in an absolute sense, without sentimentality. Perhaps the theologian Paul Tillich expressed
this best when he put it in the passive voice, saying
that in the context of this agapic philosophy you will
feel accepted for exactly who you are. You will not judge
yourself badly for your mistakes but at the deepest possible level will feel received and honored.

It strikes us when, year after year, the longed-
for perfection of life does not appear, when the
old compulsions reign within us as they have for
decades, when despair destroys all joy and courage. Sometimes at that moment a wave of light
breaks into our darkness, and it is as though a
voice were saying: "You are accepted. You are
accepted, accepted by that which is greater than
you, and the name of which you do not know.
Do not ask for the name now; perhaps you will
find it later. Do not try to do anything now; perhaps later you will do much. Do not seek for anything; do not perform anything; do not intend
anything. Simply accept the fact that you are

accepted!" If that happens to us, we experience grace. After such an experience we may not be better than before, and we may not believe more than before. But everything is transformed.[24]

And finally, the mystery of who Jesus is, impossible to say in simple and factual terms, will be revealed in the context of this spiritual and mundane agape. His very essence cannot be known intellectually—not in history and not in theology—but only by discovering the power of love and how it can operate as a basic life principle.

Perhaps this means that the more we establish the reign of love in our domestic and international contexts, the better we will understand what Jesus was all about. Until then, we grope in the dark with language that is inadequate and with forms and institutions that fail. The shift in worldview from power to love is so radical that one can hardly imagine what the change would be like in practical terms.

At the core of the Gospel philosophy of love is an appreciation of difference and respect for precisely what is "other." Agape has nothing to do with like-minded people supporting each other. Story after story tells of foreigners, aliens, and misfits being welcomed. The point is to create a world community that transcends religious allegiance and nationalism.

Let's remember once again the four key elements in the kingdom: *basilea, metanoia, therapeia,* and *agape*— kingdom, change in vision, healing, and love. All are profoundly intermingled and dependent on each other, and all are required to manifest the mystery of who Jesus was and what he was working to establish.

Like the Buddha, Jesus addressed human suffering, but his answer was not the Four Noble Truths and the

Eightfold Path; it was a vision of human life based on the four key elements I have been spelling out from the outset. It would be a new kingdom, a new plan for human existence consisting of mutual regard and the end of paranoia. It would be a place where all sorts of wounds and illnesses are healed.

CHAPTER 5

Everyone A Healer

In the Kingdom One Responds to Suffering

*Jesus called the twelve to gather and gave them power
and authority over all daimons and to heal illnesses.
He sent them to speak publicly of the kingdom of
God . . . They set out and went through the villages
spreading the good news and healing in every place.*

—Luke 9:1–2, 6

The good news is that we are creating a new world
order in which the first task is to heal each other.

The Buddha begins his teaching with the simple
observation that there is suffering in the world. Jesus
similarly focuses on the sickness of soul that affects
people individually and socially, physically and spiritually. This perception of sickness is central, and healing
is his signature activity. Jesus does not teach how to be
virtuous, how to be saved, or how to be a good church

member. He says nothing about memorizing dogma or following a strict set of moral rules. Instead, he continually demonstrates how to be in this world as a healer.

I know a Christian minister who is an instinctive healer. Everywhere he goes, he sees need when it is present. Where others overlook a person in distress, he stops to find out what is wrong. He has a Gospel instinct and knows intuitively that the role of minister is to heal.

I know several ministers who don't have this gift. It doesn't come with ordination. I do have a Buddhist friend who responds similarly, and, to my mind, his healing reactions place him in the kingdom Jesus envisioned. He is a Buddhist by affiliation, but his way of life is precisely in tune with the way Jesus taught. He found his way into the kingdom through the Buddha.

The Gospels use several words for healing, but the main one is *therapeia*, "therapy." Plato used this very word in the dialogue *Euthyphro*, where Socrates defines it as "service of the gods." When you heal, you are doing sacred work. The Gospels appeared 400 years after Plato, and yet they, too, emphasize this word *therapeia*, a word so important that it could identify the Gospel spirit wherever it appears. If you want to live the Gospel philosophy, you have to know what it takes to be a healer.

I understand that this word *healer* sometimes seems romantic, but in fact it represents a cold, clear, harsh reality. People suffer—emotionally, physically, spiritually, and relationally. They need help. From time to time we are all in need of healing, and we are all called to be healers.

There was a time in my life when I needed healing. I had just gone through a divorce. I was fired from my job as a college professor—the only career I wanted at the time and one in which I had invested years of study. I was so upset that I felt sick and sores appeared in my throat and mouth. In reaction, I became too dependent on a few close friends, and many people around me pitied me and told me, essentially, to grow up. But another friend, James Hillman, a Jewish man who had written many things critical of Christianity, visited me and gave me some food, a glass of wine, and some thoughtful, friendly counsel. I have never forgotten his generous response. From my point of view, he was a healer in the spirit of the Gospel.

Healing is an altruistic action, in the root sense of the word—other. You think about the other person's welfare. You are profoundly convivial, meaning that you "live with" others, not just for yourself. You heal because of your empathy for the suffering of the other.

In the Gospels, Jesus never frets about himself. He is always in response mode, noticing suffering of all kinds and responding to it with a healing word or touch.

The Spiritual in Illness

The sick are similar to the poor and rejected, who, Jesus says, are honored citizens in his new kingdom. Again we run into the mystery by which the afflicted have a special entry into the kingdom. They are not in an ordinary, unconscious condition. Illness has taken them out of default reality and put them in a liminal place. They are somewhere between life and death and are therefore ready for the kingdom.

Illness makes you aware of your dependence on other people, the fragility of your life, and your mortality. Quite naturally it inspires you to ask the great questions: *What is important? What does it mean? Where can I turn for help?*

Illness is a spur to consciousness, and, as the religion scholar Mircea Eliade says, it is an initiation. You can look at illness purely as misfortune, as something gone wrong, but without denying any pain and suffering, you can also see it as a turning point and even an opportunity. Illness is the tunnel you go through on your way to a new level of awareness. That dark tunnel is also a birth canal.

It isn't the body alone that gets sick. Some illnesses manifest a sickness at heart, an emotional failure or setback. Some reveal a failure in spirituality and meaning. Even those illnesses that seem to come from genetic issues, organ weakness, or pollution or contagion affect the entire person and so are amenable to spiritual intervention.

In the context of modern science and technology, Jesus' way of dealing with illness may seem strange. With a word or touch he banishes the illness as though it were an invading spirit. He doesn't treat sickness as a problem of microbes or physiology, but as a spiritual condition.

Jesus' way of healing is sometimes explained as a response to problems that are psychosomatic (the body affected by the psyche) or psychogenic (illness caused by the psyche), a modern way of making sense of his healing powers. But the Gospels ask us to reimagine illness and healing as involving soul and spirit. Perhaps we, too, could heal miraculously if we addressed the whole person in this way.

For two years I visited Saint Francis Hospital in Hartford, Connecticut, monthly as a consultant. With a chaplain and the hospital's head of integrative medicine, I interviewed workers in all parts of the hospital, as well as patients and their families. Everywhere I heard people say that this hospital stood out for its special attention to patients. Patients told me that they always felt like real persons, individuals, and not just another body to take care of. I asked about the source of this special attitude and was told about the Catholic sisters from France who founded the hospital. I read their story and found that they were simply implementing the Gospel teaching. They were being healers and not just technicians.

As a therapist, I have seen many people get better physically and in every other way just through intimate and open conversation. I don't judge them, and I don't tell them how they should live. I listen to them and in their suffering welcome them into the human race. We all suffer. I help them get a perspective on their pain, and I laugh with them about how we complain and wish for an ideal life. I have no doubt that the body can be healed by spiritual compassion.

Spiritual Melodrama

Jesus' approach to healing, taken superficially, translates into a kind of "faith healing" that has convinced many followers to focus on melodramatic cures rather than simple care of the sick. Let's digress for a moment and consider it more closely.

The word *melodrama* means drama with music, melody, and soaring violins in the background. It involves emotions and situations that are exaggerated yet empty. We turn religion into melodrama when we detach it from genuine life and stuff it with inflated vocabulary and grand gestures. Melodrama rises from the combination of worthlessness and extravagance.

When we relieve the Jesus figure of its melodrama, the way is clear to show how his teaching applies to real life. Agapic healing is not a flashy display of superhuman powers that impress and convince; it is a thoughtful, grounded effort to relieve suffering and deal with disease. It might be more appropriate to convince a corporation not to pollute a river that supplies water to families and children than to put on shows of magical cures. The real miracle is to convince those in power to live by agape and then to enjoy a healthy world.

So, when we talk about Jesus as healer, we might emphasize healing of body, soul, and spirit rather than the superhuman flair of his methods. He doesn't ask that we bow down in worship before his powers of healing but rather that we find our own ways of doing the same. In every case his healing is motivated by compassion rather than a desire to impress. He models how to be responsive to a community in its distress.

Healing Persons, Not Cases

Jesus' mode of healing was consistent with the kingdom of heaven and not with contemporary ideas of medical science. Some try to reduce one to the other, explaining his "miraculous" cures in modern terms. An alternative is to step outside the circle of modernism and appreciate a different world order altogether, a realm that is not limited to materialistic methods and explanations. There, body, soul, and spirit are intertwined, and healing involves the whole person.

When Jesus heals, he usually places the healing within the full context of life. After curing a blind man, he utters mysterious words: "I came into this world for a decision—so that the blind see and those who see become blind" (John 9:36).

Like the shift from power to love that we looked at in the last chapter, to Jesus, curing the blind is actually all about worldview and understanding. Your vision is restored so that you can see what life is all about. He opens your eyes to a better world and closes them to the self-destructive ways that you take for granted. What needs cure is the inner eye by which we make sense of the world.

Today, we don't trust the mind or imagination much, preferring to treat illness with mechanical or chemical tools. But Jesus knows that our ideas and images can make us sick. The way we understand the world leads to a style of living that can make us ill. It makes sense that a shift in mentality could heal.

Jesus heals by clearing out the demonic, forgiving misdeeds, and rewarding trust. Confronted with illness, he sees a failed experiment in life or the intrusion of a spiritual error. He encourages people to trust, to change their ways, and to embrace the vision of the kingdom—all aspects of healing.

Healing as Nourishment

> *Jesus said to them, "I am the bread of life.*
> *Whoever comes to me will never be hungry*
> *and whoever trusts me will never be thirsty."*

> —JOHN 6:35

These key words of Jesus demonstrate that he wants to be heard poetically rather than literally. Jesus is not actual bread. Listening to these words, you don't stock up your pantry with baked goods. Rather, his way of being, his vision and teachings, is the basic nutrient of your soul and spirit. If you do as he does, your soul and spirit will be fed. Today, we understand that the food we take into our bodies affects our health. What we don't appreciate is that the soul and spirit also require proper nourishment. Taking in bad ideas and cultivating a dehumanizing vision leads to a sickness of soul and spirit, a sickness that invades our personal lives and society as a whole.

It's odd, given the emphasis in the Gospels on healing, that followers of Jesus talk so much about being saved. They call Jesus the savior rather than the healer. It isn't clear just what "saved" means. In an old-fashioned theology of hellfire, it might mean protected from eternal torment. In a more existential reading, it could mean saved from meaninglessness or from a wasted, unconscious life. Still, I would rather replace roadside signs that say "Jesus Saves" with "Jesus Heals."

Soul sickness is related to but different from physical illness. A person of considerable financial or political power may be overcome by a need to control and to put others down—using people as a stepladder to success. We may see this attitude as immoral or as a sign of a bad character but not as sickness. A person may embezzle, cheat, pollute, destroy, and lie his way to the top. Eventually we may put him in prison, but we won't see the sickness in his soul. Worse, if we did see it, we wouldn't know what to do with it.

A moralistic attitude, which is yet another by-product of materialism and egotism, sees everything in terms of black and white, good and bad. It fills court-rooms and builds prisons instead of clinics and hospitals. It is blind to the complexities of a life. Because it believes it perceives evil clearly, it can make laws for every complicated aspect of human life and then punish those who break the laws, irrespective of their motives and emotional stability. It can't distinguish between bad behavior and sickness of soul.

A moral attitude is quite different. It considers the conditions under which people make bad decisions and dally with criminality and resort to violence. It sorts out the context of bad behavior and tries to heal conflicted emotions, twisted histories, and misguided views. Rather than punish individuals, it works toward a healed society.

Spiritually Empty, Yet Blessed

> *Blessed, the utterly poor in spirit, for*
> *the kingdom of heaven is given to them.*
>
> —MATTHEW 5:3

It is difficult to understand this beatitude. Why should the poor in spirit be blessed? And what does it mean, anyway, to be poor in spirit? Does it mean to live in the spirit of poverty without necessarily being literally poor? Or does it refer to spiritual emptiness—nonattachment, openness, and lack of rigidity?

It could refer to a spirit of simplicity or it might be close to what the Zen master calls *sunyata,* emptiness, the utter openness of mind and heart praised in the much-loved Heart Sutra of Buddhism. According to the Heart Sutra, achieving the state of spiritual emptiness ushers directly into Nirvana, a word not that far distant from the Greek word used in the beatitudes: *makarioi,* the blissful beatitude of the gods, who, the *Iliad* says, are free from the struggles that occupy humans. The poor in spirit are in this blissful condition of the gods. "Blessed" here means not only gifted and graced but godly, high in the realm of spirit, on the far reaches of human imagination.

If you are suffering the existential anxiety of trying to make sense of life in a complex world, that anxiety may translate into both emotional and physical illness. Your way out of suffering is to reimagine and reinvent your life. That is what Jesus is all about: reinventing your worldview so that you become less paranoid and narcissistic—two neuroses typical of the materialistic and corporate structures of modern life—and unleash the creative power of agape, a base of human interaction that is loving rather than competitive and power-driven.

Jesus was closer to the Buddha than to the modern doctor when he healed those many that came to him pleading for his care. His first business was to address the state of their souls, and in doing so he healed them in body as well. He was not a miracle worker as much as a healer far ahead of his time. One day we may understand the connection between meaning, emotion, and health and better appreciate the unusual attitude of the Gospels toward healing.

Describing the point of view of the healing Buddha, the Venerable Thrangu Rinpoche says, "The fundamental cause of sickness and suffering is a lack of contentment and the addictive quality of samsara." This profound statement is completely in tune with the Gospel Jesus. For contentment, we tend to use the word *happiness,* but that's not quite right. Epicurus used *tranquility,* which can be misconstrued as passivity. Jesus says "bliss" in the beatitudes. They all apply: when we are deeply discontent, unhappy, lacking tranquility, and far from bliss, the soul is in a sad and sickened state. And since body and soul are inseparable, the body shows its discontent in disease and organ failure.

Hospice workers sometimes say that a person was healed but not cured. I remember one woman, a neighbor and friend, who died of lung cancer. For weeks she was frantically running from doctor to doctor looking for a cure for her disease. Finally, she realized that she was going to die. One day she came to me calm and relatively cheerful. "I'm not going to be cured," she said sadly, "but I'm healed."

Healed Through Trust

When he entered Capernaum, a centurion approached him, making a request. "Sir," he said, "my servant is at home lying paralyzed and suffering badly." Jesus said to him, "I will go and care for him."

The centurion answered, "Sir, I'm not worthy to have you under my roof. Just speak, and my servant will be cured. For I, too, am a person with authority and have soldiers under me. I say to one of them "Go," and he goes, and to another "Come," and he comes, and to my servant "Do this," and he does it.

When Jesus heard this, he was amazed and told those who were following him: "I'm telling you, I have not discovered this kind of trust in Israel."

Jesus said to the centurion, "Go. What you have put trust in will be done." His servant was cured in that very hour.

—MATTHEW 8:5–10, 13

In the story of the centurion, which has moved people for hundreds of years, Jesus points out two qualities of soul that prepare a person for the kingdom: trust and humility. The soldier impresses Jesus with his deep trust and with his appreciation for Jesus' authority. The occupying officer acknowledges the superiority of a wandering teacher.

Again, we see a reversal of expectations. The centurion might be the last person you would expect to be a good candidate for the kingdom of heaven. But his faith and humility are so deeply felt that they move Jesus to action. Followers of Jesus are invited, as usual, to adopt the same attitude: noticing the authority of someone who by any external measure would be an inferior but whose character demands respect.

In the context of Jesus' work to create a new kind of community for humankind, this cure also suggests that to be a member you don't have to belong to any particular group. It's the outsider, the questionable person, the one under suspicion who has the better chance. What we think is proper and acceptable might not be at all a ticket to the kingdom. This constant and essential theme of the Gospels is worth keeping in mind as you forge a Jesus spirituality.

The history of spirituality shows that the archetype of spirit, the experience of being seized by a longing to get more out of life and finding a home for your spirituality, often leads to the sense of being chosen. Whether in an established religion or in a small spiritual community, people may feel that they are right and the others wrong, they are special and the rest of humanity is unlucky. Jesus' teaching goes in the opposite direction. It is in those moments when you feel you don't belong and can't fit in and are no longer worthy of being included that the kingdom is near.

Followers of Jesus could make a startling and radical move closer to the kingdom if only they could see the wisdom in the story of the centurion. Jesus did not come to establish a club of elite believers. He came to make of the entire world population a community of people focused on overcoming their narcissism and egotism.

Like the centurion's servant, we would be healed, if we transcended the infantile and neurotic need to be above those who are not in our club. For "club," substitute church, spiritual community, or body of believers. Imagine Jesus as speaking to the people of the world, not to convert them to a theology or, worse, an ideology, but to persuade them to mature spiritually, to arrive at a point of civility and imagination that allows them to live in peace and under the rule of agape.

To heal is not just to get rid of disease but to waken and revivify a person who has become soul-dead. The connection between soul issues and physical symptoms is mysterious, at least at this point in time. I expect that in 200 years or so we will be more sophisticated about this tie-in. For now, we split soul and body and fail to understand at all what Jesus was doing as a healer.

If you are healthy, body, soul, and spirit, you will not be preoccupied with yourself or judge others out of desperate anxiety about your own moral confusion. Health is the state of well-being that comes from being free of these neurotic tensions. It is a condition of love, creativity, and connection.

Jesus places health of soul and spirit first; physical cure follows. What does it mean to be sick in soul and spirit? A sick soul is what you bring to a psychotherapist. Your relationships are in trouble. You may be depressed or feel paranoid. You may express your fragile soul in overeating, smoking, and gambling. Psychology is fairly accurate in telling us how the soul gets sick, though it rarely uses the word *soul*.

It's unusual to talk about a sick spirit, but it is a very serious problem. You may have an infantile notion of God, afterlife, morality, and belief. Your spiritual ideas may not have changed since you were a child. You may be rigid and judgmental in your moral positions—notice the problems of the religious leaders that Jesus challenges. You may be caught up in the materialistic life of the times and fail to understand the importance of caring for your spiritual life. You may translate your need for transcendence and religion into sports and money and adventure. Many of the problems of the world are due to spirit gone amok.

We speak of body, soul, and spirit as though they were separate entities, but in life they are three sides of a single triangle. When you are sick in one, the others suffer. You can't heal one without giving attention to the others, though contemporary society keeps it all separate. Jesus addresses all three in each of his healings and so gives us a crucial lesson in the meaning of health.

If we were to follow through on Jesus' example of healing, our hospitals would look quite different. Now, we tend to put spiritual issues on the side or at the bottom of the list, if at all. We could instead address the whole person from the beginning of treatment, including the spiritual issues of meaning, vision, values, and the sense of transcendence.

Every significant illness is an intimation of our mortality. It reminds us that we aren't going to live forever, and that realization is a spiritual crisis whenever it appears. What is life all about? How does death make sense? What's the use of trying so hard if it's all going to end? These are spiritual questions that arise either explicitly or subliminally in every illness.

Several times, Jesus tells his students to emulate him and go out healing. It is the characteristic activity of the kingdom. That could mean that anyone wishing to adopt the Jesus spirituality would find ways to heal whenever physical, spiritual, or emotional sickness comes along. Teachers could help heal their students. Manufacturers could make objects that in no way make people sick and in fact contribute to their customers' health and welfare. Bankers and accountants could keep in mind the various sicknesses of soul related to money, and politicians could do everything possible, before all else, to keep their constituents healthy and give them access to health care.

The student of Jesus never forgets the charge to care for souls, to be a healer in every sense of the word. But to be a healer is not exactly the same as healing people who are sick. It is less a matter of doing and more of being. To be a healer you have to be transformed as a person, transfigured by your new and different outlook on humanity and the world.

CHAPTER 6

—FACE YOUR DEMONS

How to be Healed of That Which Possesses Us

He invited his twelve students to be with him and gave them the authority to expel disturbing spirits and to heal [therapeuein] every illness and disease.

—MATTHEW 10:1

As Jesus walked the roads of Galilee, he demonstrated powers that seem remote from an ordinary person's life: calming the sea, healing disease with a word or gesture, and casting out demons, which today sounds like something from a Gothic horror tale. Strange images out of bizarre movies come to mind: objects fly through the air; sickening gurgles and screams issue from the mouths of innocent children; an old priest in a black serge cassock flies in from Rome at midnight to exorcise a haunted house.[25] But Jesus was not a character in a horror movie.

He lived a thoughtful life, demonstrating what it would be like to enjoy a godly[26] existence.

Dealing with the demonic is part of that existence—an extension of the healing we discussed in the last chapter, one of the four basic activities of the Jesus way. The question is, what does that mean today, when we don't speak seriously about it? How do we ordinary people banish demons?

The Demonic in Contemporary Life

We human beings have a demonic streak that gives rise to rage, jealousy, and violent conflict. Have you ever been consumed by the desire for an illicit lover, felt envy toward a co-worker, or wanted someone you know to fail? Have you ever felt overcome by jealousy or hatred? Have you ever felt this so strongly that it seemed as though another person inhabited you? People say about someone in such a state, "That man is crazy! He's possessed!"

In many ways possession is like obsession. Something gets hold of you, and you lose your free will. In spite of all your efforts to the contrary, you focus on this one thing and can't be released from it. Sometimes the object of your fascination would horrify you if you were in your right mind. There are famous cases of mothers so obsessed with evil that they killed their children to purify them and afterward couldn't tolerate the memory of the deed.

But possession is a step beyond obsession. You feel taken over by a presence so strong that your usual self seems to have disappeared. Murderers sometimes say,

"Something came over me." Psychotic people, who may exhibit passions that ordinary men and women feel to a lesser degree, sometimes hallucinate literal demons that possess them. They may know their names and recognize them in their comings and goings, and they feel powerless in the face of their demands. Part of the pain in psychosis comes from the sense of being subjugated.

Possession is not just a state of anxiety, and Jesus was not merely a master therapist. He wasn't curing mental illness but expurgating the demonic. Psychology concerns itself with the emotional response to being possessed; Jesus faced the demonic head-on and was able to heal a person by ridding him of the demonic influence that controlled him. If jealousy is ruining your life, you have to arrive at deep-seated realization about who you are and what life is about before that demon will depart. If envy is giving you violent thoughts, you have to change the way you see things before it will leave you alone. If greed consumes you, you have to face this adversary to be free of it.

I have seen the demonic get hold of a person and banish all self-awareness. One mild example: There was a man I knew, though not well, who wrote a book on nature. At about the same time, I wrote a book that had several chapters on nature. When he read my book, he became inflamed. He was certain that I had stolen ideas from him. In fact, I had never read a sentence he had written.

He wrote me a mean-spirited letter threatening to sue me for extravagant sums of money. I was making a living with my writing, while he felt frustrated that he couldn't find a big publisher. I had the feeling that he was possessed. He wasn't his normal self. I tried to reason with him, but that was impossible, because I was dealing with something demonic.

Jesus understands that the demonic is implicated in illness. In one story of exorcism, Jesus cures a man who has convulsions. Today, we say, "Oh, that man wasn't possessed. He had epilepsy or some other kind of seizure." We feel superior with our abstractions, but the people around Jesus may have had an awareness that we have lost—the sense that we are persons within persons. The feelings that overwhelm us may be felt as separate, interior personalities at work behind the façade we present to the world.

Usually these inner figures remain in the background, and we experience them as passions and urges that are present but don't overpower us. But there are times in the lives of most people when they come out of hiding. If you could stop and think for a moment when you feel driven or compelled, you might be able to give a face to that strong feeling. It might be the face of someone you have known, some aspect of yourself you recognize, or it may be a complete stranger.

I once knew a religion teacher who was highly respected in his community but had an overwhelming compulsion to expose himself. He knew he risked his reputation and livelihood with his behavior, and he detested himself for doing it. But he couldn't stop. I suspected that this demonic force in him was connected to his strict religious upbringing—a powerful, repressed sexuality so potent that it took the form of a personality over which he had no control.

Some people are haunted by other deep and powerful negative images from their past—a remembered cruelty, a sexual betrayal, or a withholding or withdrawal of love. As they grow older, they may glimpse the influence of these painful memories and then try to deal with them. At this point the struggle may become so intense that the inner demonic forces begin to show themselves as voices or even faint presences. They may actually make demands and give orders.

Possession may also arise as part of a spiritual journey. Mystics from many traditions describe how much courage they needed to deal with the strong forces that seemed to stand in the way of their spiritual advancement, like guardians at the gate. People who have seen or heard the demons that haunt them describe them as inhumanly fierce and demanding.

No one has described this process more precisely than C. G. Jung.[27] He was not speaking just theoretically; he had gone through profound struggles in which his own demons showed themselves. He even knew their names. For this he is sometimes dismissed as a troubled or even psychotic man, but it's quite clear from his writing that he was involved in intense spiritual processes, certainly tied to his personal past, that affected him deeply.

In response, Jung practiced a kind of primal simplicity, like that found in the life of Jesus, by building a tower without water and electricity where he could work on himself and his writing, by living by a lake and frequently sailing on it, and by remaining close to his thoughts and dreams. From this way of life he developed an authority, like that of Jesus, over his own demons and those of his patients.

Jesus the Exorcist

As Jesus went about Galilee teaching and healing, people came to him with their demonic issues. It was said that he cast out seven demons from Mary Magdalene. In one instance, Jesus cast out a demon from a man who was mute. After the man astonished the crowd by speaking, some said that, if he could cast out demons, Jesus himself must be demonic. Jesus responded, "If I drive out demons by the finger of God, then the kingdom of God has come to you" (Luke 11:20).

The finger of God. Michelangelo recalled this traditional image when he painted the Sistine Chapel at the Vatican. There you behold, in one of the most famous scenes, God and Adam, creator and created, their outstretched fingers almost touching. The divine and the human are electrically close in that moment of creation, but that scene has a shadow side: the human and the demonic so close that their fingers, too, almost touch. The demons poke through with a terrible autonomy to drive a person to wild fear or uncontrollable passion.[28]

Jesus refers to himself as a son of God and a son of man. In him, the New Adam, the great mystery of the spiritual and the human plays out fully. He is that point where the two fingers meet, and it is the combination of his human compassion and his spiritual power that allows him to relieve people of the demonic. Mysteriously, he can unleash a force for good equal to any demonic possession, and the people around him are always amazed at it.

If we pursue the Jesus way, we, too, are called to be exorcists, to deal courageously with the demonic forces that threaten us and our world. There is no need to be naïve about this. I am not suggesting any return to traditional rites of exorcism. Instead we should realize, once again, that human life is a battleground of forces both divine and demonic. Traditional societies dramatize this profound conflict in their vivid stories and histrionic rituals. The frightening, grotesque masks they wear in ecstatic dances, the entrancing drumming and shrieking, and the shocking rituals full of sexual and funereal images make the demonic uncomfortably real. But in our materialism and our mild, rationalistic psychologies, we see only the surfaces. That is why Jesus' statement is so important: to deal effectively with the demonic, we need God's finger, a sense of the divine.

Notice in the brief passage about the finger of God that Jesus once again connects exorcism with the kingdom. If you live the life of the kingdom, the way presented in the Gospels, you will be able to deal with the demonic. We tend to see the demon in Hitler, Al Qaeda, and communism, but we fail to notice it in our own religious literalism, our extreme nationalism and patriotism, and our aggressive treatment of our children and spouses. But it is there, and the only way to get rid of it is to acknowledge our darkness and achieve such a level of self-understanding that we have the strength and authority to resist it.

Possession and Self-Possession

Jesus is extraordinarily self-possessed, a curious word considering that we've been talking about a different kind of possession. He can be angry and sharp with his words, but even then he never seems overwhelmed by his emotions. When other people might be deeply upset, he keeps his demeanor cool. His ever-ready spiritual part keeps his human temper even.

The self-possessed person has a measure of protection from onslaughts that come from within and without. He is not so loosely put together that the slightest siren call from advertising or politics can throw him off guard. He can also feel for others, while a person who is not self-possessed can only think about himself. The self-possessed person knows who he is, what he needs, and what he can do. The possessed person is essentially and comprehensively clueless. He doesn't know what he wants because he is riddled with demonic desires. He doesn't believe he has any power, because the demons are controlling him.

Self-possession is not the same as self-control. You possess yourself when you are able to allow life to flow through you. You are not threatened, and you do not resist. You are a conduit for the uncertainties that life offers you. You possess yourself because you are not fighting the life that wants to be in you.

Self-possession offers enormous power, and Jesus seems to have had it in great measure. He is comfortable speaking with people whose lives have been wrecked by the demonic, and he stands firm in the face of the wildest forms of possession. Out of his personal evenness he draws on his spiritual power to realign the demonic so that it isn't overwhelming.

The Gospel says that people were astonished at the authority with which Jesus commanded demonic spirits to leave possessed people. Authority is a curious quality to focus on. And yet, when we are possessed, it's true that we have no authority in our lives. We feel fully taken over by whatever has entered us and are subject to it.

Jesus takes most of his authority from his constant and direct connection to his heavenly or archetypal father, a paternal spirit that gives him the power and confidence to face the demonic. The father spirit works through him, so that, as he says, when you look at him, you see the father. The constant connection to the father is what expands his vision and enables the compassion that makes him a healer.

After centuries of literalism and naïve conceptions of God the Father, it is difficult to get an intelligent and grounded sense of who or what the father is and to understand, let alone adopt Jesus' devotion. Perhaps we may think of it as devotion to destiny, a sense of world order and governance, and a willingness to let life flow through you, unencumbered by the limitations of your will and intention. Most spiritual teachings recommend being in accord with a larger source of meaning and vitality, to live less by the tight control of will and more by yielding to meaning as it reveals itself. From this perspective, the father spirit can be glimpsed in the intelligence and beauty of creation and in the unfolding of individual lives.

Once you get away from the naïve notion of the father spirit, you can see the sense in those scenes in the Gospels where Jesus ascribes his power and authority to the father. He is open to a life force greater than his own. He is a conduit rather than the producer of power, and this spiritual attitude, consistent and intense, is the essence of his religiousness. If there is anything religious about Jesus' conduct, it is his faithful acknowledgment of a power beyond himself.

Jesus' relation to his father demonstrates how a high spiritual outlook helps deal with intense emotions and neurotic and psychotic misperceptions of reality. From that higher perspective you can be confident as you challenge the blind passions and suppressed urges that overwhelm you. When I want to be clear to myself about God as father, I recall the prayer that Black Elk, the famous American Indian holy man, taught: "O Father and Grandfather Wakan-Tanka, You are the source and end of everything. My father Wakan-Tanka, You are the One who watches over and sustains all life."[29]

Exorcism, Not Repression

Some would argue that Jesus' habit of casting out demons means that he did not appreciate the dark side of life, that he was moralistic and lopsided in his goodness. Many who follow him reinforce that misconception by dividing life into good and evil and then waging a war against evil. But Jesus' exorcisms were done in the name of healing and not as part of a moral crusade.

A person who is possessed is in great pain. You catch it in her dark, distracted eyes. You hear it in her edgy voice. You see it in her physical posture and mannerisms. The possession is not just mental and emotional. It snakes its way into the body and into relationships. It can be profoundly disruptive. In this sense, it is something to be healed, not fought.

In one remarkable passage, the Gospel tells how Jesus encountered a man who had been possessed and went around naked and slept in tombs. Jesus spoke directly to the demons in the man: "What is your name?" he asked. "Legion," the man shouted. The demons begged Jesus not to cast them into the abyss but instead send them into a herd of pigs. At Jesus' command, they left the man and entered the pigs, which rushed down into a lake and were drowned. Afterward, the man sat calmly at Jesus' feet, dressed and in his right mind.

Today, you might ask someone, "Do you have an inner demon?" If the person were honest, he would probably say, "I have many inner demons." That is the answer the possessed man gave, and it is true of us all. We have many demonic urges driving us from one minute to the next, though one may be pressing at any particular time. They may be the demons of anger, pride, insecurity, longing, and grief, or even of some seemingly quite different force, such as creativity.

The Greeks of old were careful with their use of this word *demon*. They spoke instead of a *daimon,* a spirit that made one feel driven or possessed but could be either good or bad. Socrates referred to love as a daimon. In the story of Legion, the Gospel uses this same Greek word *daimon,* which is probably best not translated as "demon" at all. A sentence or two before, it calls the daimons "unclean spirits," suggesting that the spirits that haunt us are not all unclean. Some people do seem to be possessed, for example, by the creative daimon or by the desire to do good.

In this sense, Jesus is not attacking evil as such, and so the tales of exorcism don't have to be understood in a context of good versus evil but more of self-possession versus madness. Imagine the forces that make you feel driven, whatever they are, departing suddenly, leaving you feeling self-possessed. These forces may have felt so real and independent that you can actually imagine them rushing off into some other object. I knew a woman who told me that when she got into a real rage about her family, she would bake bread and feed them with it. She drove the demons into the bread, and this mild form of exorcism—less dramatic but much like that of Jesus—relieved her.

Today we use drugs, talk therapy, incarceration, and behavior modification in an attempt to quell the most destructive demonic presences in society. But it would be much better to rediscover the secret of Jesus the exorcist and approach the demonic with the authority that comes from having dealt with our narcissism, paranoia, and aggression.

In the Biblical story of Lucifer, the demon in him is split off from the angel. Our demons, too, have destructive power because they are divided. Maybe the demon of alcoholism wouldn't possess us if we could reconnect with the angel daimon of Dionysian joy. Maybe the demon of materialism would depart if we discovered the real joy of living in a beautiful and wondrous material world. Maybe the demon of sex wouldn't lead so many into abusing others if its positive side was allowed to exercise its power.

Daimon becomes demon when it is not given a place in life, when we do everything possible not to be contaminated by the strong spirit of, say, sexuality or abandon. In this way, religion based on virtue colludes with the demonic. What is needed is another approach, the one offered in the Gospels: face the daimon with all its contradictions and threats and find passion there rather than virtue.

Jesus did not divide people simplistically into the good and the bad. He predicted that Peter would betray him, and yet he made Peter a prominent leader in his group. He kindly accepted Thomas, who was full of doubt about him, and later, according to tradition, Thomas became a major spokesman for the Jesus life in the East. Jesus overruled the judgment of his friends against the woman with the alabaster jar, who anointed him with expensive oils.

This capacity to see the value in every kind of person, of every level in society, from any place on earth, and with any problem or neurosis imaginable, is central to Jesus' character and philosophy and his way of walking through life. Every day you encounter people you haven't met before and situations that may be unfamiliar. It may seem wise and proper to stay close to your principles and the people you know and trust, but Jesus is more of a social adventurer. He seems to enjoy the differences among people and to present himself as a paradox.

Living in paradox, being open to life's variety, not judging, walking slowly and attentively through life, offering love and kindness in the most combative conditions—these basic qualities offer power over the demonic. You don't have to know secret mantras and blessings. You don't have to resort to electroconvulsive therapy. You don't have to be a believer. All you have to do is walk attentively and acceptingly through life.

Facing the Demonic

At the personal level, facing the demonic means, first, acknowledging its presence. If you sense a deep and chronic anger in you and notice it slipping out in moments of rage, know that there is a demonic force in you that needs attention and has to be dealt with authoritatively. This can be difficult to recognize, because the demonic often presents, as traditional stories of the devil often say, in a positive light. Your patriotism and nationalism may seem of great value to you, so you fail to notice how they possess you and cause you to bring harm to others. The intensity of your love may seem altogether virtuous to you, but to your partner or lover it shows itself as possessiveness or dangerous jealousy.

The demonic in you needs to be addressed boldly and then purged. The Jesus way is not to defend against it, look for blame, or explain it but to face it directly and release it. This sort of exorcism is not the melodramatic kind but rather a strong and authoritative refusal to be taken over. In this form, exorcism involves a deep shift in perspective, perhaps the most difficult thing a person can achieve.

Martin Luther King, Jr., confronted the demon of racism thoughtfully, boldly, and courageously. He spoke with the authority of one who had studied enough, seen enough, reflected enough to cut through any rationalizations that might shield racism as well as any violent counter efforts that themselves bordered on the demonic. He was an exorcist for an entire society.

People whose lives have been torn apart by the demon of alcohol know how difficult it is to "cast out" this debilitating presence. Decisions and resolutions are not enough. You have to summon up the strength, perhaps get help from others, and find it in you to choose to live your life rather than to be dominated by temptation.

You don't just call on Jesus in a naïve and infantile manner. You learn from his example and spiritual intelligence how to develop the authority you need to overcome the spirit that possesses you. You may have to deal with your memories, your continuing anger, and your frustrations. You may have to learn how to open your heart without fear and live the philosophy of agape that is central to the Gospels. You may have to find a conduit to the source of your life, an abiding spiritual awareness that brings you up out of the small perimeters of your mind and your life. Knowing your power, you stand up to the demons and recover your spiritual health.

CHAPTER 7

TRANSFIGURATION AND METAMORPHOSIS

The Go-Between of Worlds

*They asked him, "What sign will you make so
we can trust you? What will you do? Our fathers
ate manna in the desert, according to what was
written: 'He gave them bread from heaven to eat.'"*

*"I'm telling you," said Jesus. "It wasn't Moses who
gave you the bread from heaven; it's my father who gives
you the true bread from heaven. For the bread of God
is what comes down from heaven and gives life to the
world. Whoever comes to me will never be hungry, and
whoever has faith in me will never be thirsty."*

—John 6:30–35

At the last supper, Jesus uttered a few mysterious
words that resound through the centuries: "This is my

body." Apparently he was referring to a piece of bread that he would share with his friends and students. But how could a piece of bread be his body? I grew up thinking that the bread of communion was magical, but real, flesh, so real that when I took it into my mouth I felt I shouldn't bite it with my teeth.

When Jesus says, "This [the bread] is my body," clearly he refers to his presence as a person. He isn't referring to a corpse, to a purely physical entity. He means that bread is, mysteriously, who he is. Something about his nature is akin to bread.

The Greek language has several words for the body. For example, *sarx* means flesh and *soma,* the word used in this passage, usually means a living body or a body of people or the physical aspect as distinguished from the spiritual. Yet, as a good Catholic, I grew up thinking of the bread of the Eucharist as sarx and communion as somehow eating the flesh. This is entirely different from incorporating in a physical way, through bread, the substance of who Jesus was.

He had already said, "I am the bread of life." In the passage quoted above, he compares his bread with that of Moses and says that it is "true" bread coming from the father. We saw in our discussion of baptism that alchemists distinguished plain water from "eternal water," which is a spiritual substance that they also refer to as *aqua vera* or true water. It affects the soul primarily and the body only ritually.

In a similar way, the true bread is bread in a spiritual sense. It comes from the father, Jesus says, to give the world life. In the context of the kingdom, that life must be more than plain physical existence. It would be the kind of life Jesus discussed with Nicodemus, a new kind of living, a deeper vitality that arises when you are in accord with the desires of the father.

Just as plain bread sustains the physical body as one of its primary foods, so Jesus' teaching and example sustain the soul and spirit. It is one thing to have a radical change of heart and another to sustain it. Bread, the nourishing staple of Jesus' teaching, is sustenance.

Bread from heaven is obviously different from earthly bread. But the two kinds of bread have something in common: they nourish and sustain. Among the nutrients of life, they are basic. If you are going to sustain your higher vision and the ideals of the kingdom, you need to feed yourself daily in an appropriate way. The "food" you need is Jesus himself: his teachings, his example, and his stories. For all of this the main Gospel image is bread.

In his descriptions of the true bread in John, in what is sometimes referred to as the Bread of Life Discourse, Jesus says several times that this bread brings life to the world and satisfies a spiritual hunger. The vitality he is speaking of is not just physical existence, not just breathing but being alive as a thinking, imagining, relating human being. Obviously, a person can be physically vital and yet spiritually dead. Jesus as bread keeps the spirit and soul in the peak of health.

The Poetry of Bread

From the beginning, students of Jesus have gathered to share holy bread called Eucharist, meaning thanks, thanks for the new life made possible by the new image for mankind presented in the Gospels. They look at the bread and treat it as immensely holy, because it is, for now, the presence of Jesus. Something of his essence is manifested in that bread, just as leaven signifies the dynamic of the kingdom. The Jesus vision is like yeast that makes life rise.

They eat the bread, so that not only the food but the act of eating has meaning in the spiritual poetics of the kingdom. You take this kingdom into you. You chew it and make it part of yourself. You incorporate it, digest it, and are nourished by it. You become a different kind of being: transparent, translucent, spiritually alive, visionary, and profoundly communal.

Jesus is not present physically now in bodily form. Now the bread of the communal meal, which dramatizes the core teaching about community and agape, is the physical manifestation of his being, just as his personal body once was. The bread is now his body, the wine his blood, and eating and drinking a further dimension of the process by which Jesus is made ever present.

The point of this lasting bread, as he says several times in the Bread of Life Discourse, is to bring vitality to the world, to wake it up and get it going. Culture can be frenetic in its various activities and yet at the same time remain soul-dead. Jesus offers a teaching that will keep the soul and spirit alive and well.

Years ago, when I was still naïve and studying theology, the question came up in a class: could a priest go into a bakery and transform all the bread there into the body of Jesus? We understood that a priest alone has the power to change ordinary bread into the bread of life.

At the time, the question was a real puzzle for me. The priest had the power, but the whole scenario didn't seem right. I couldn't find an answer to the conundrum.

Today, I would say that when you go to a restaurant with friends and pass bread around, you could be remembering the example of Jesus and evoking the bread of life. Gathering friends around a table, as at the last supper, is a key symbolic action in the Gospel spirit. You are creating community, beginning with the intimate community of friends.

Ritual as Play

In some ways Jesus was a comic figure, a sacred comedian, and much of what he says and does is full of play. It isn't the kind of play that is raucous and obvious. His wit is subtle, more thought-provoking than broadly humorous.

When Jesus says that the bread is his body and tells his friends to eat the bread, there is a kind of serious play going on. In the last chapter, I told you about a very feisty and bright woman who, when she got angry at her family, baked her "demons" into bread, kneading the dough with all her might. She forced all her thoughts and emotions into the bread, and then, when the family ate it, she took great pleasure knowing that they were taking in her strong feelings.

Some people would no doubt be offended by my referring to ritual as play. They might think I mean "play" in the sense of only playing around, not important. But I'm thinking of play more philosophically. Many of the things we do seriously are in a certain sense play. Government diplomacy has a clear sense of play: formal parties filled with language not to be taken literally. Business, with its competition and ploys, has the quality of a game. Religious ritual is serious, maybe the most serious of all, and yet it has many aspects of play. The leaders, for example, dress up and engage in elaborate pageantry and follow strict rubrics to create a scenario, only it's one that has to do with soul and spirit rather than practical life.

Religions play with the body to make absolutely serious points about the fate of the soul. In India, the human body is given seven spiritual centers, or chakras, each representing a different quality of soul, from the anal base to the top of the head, which opens to eternity. This is playing with the body in a serious way, giving it meaning and a ritual. In sex, too, the body is the focus of play. In carvings at the famous Indian temples at Khajuraho and Konark, couples in various styles of embrace represent the erotic connections of life.

The body as bread also arises from the serious play of the imagination. Children have fun eating a gingerbread man. Artist Janine Antoni has created busts of herself out of soap and chocolate. She once watched her carefully made sculptures dissolve in the bathtub and then had the idea of licking the chocolate. She saw the work as both serious and humorous, and she even noticed the connection to the Eucharist, a link I am developing here.

You look at food given human shape, and you play with the sense that it is real. It is easy to let the imagination move between worlds, one serious and one playful, one physical and one spiritually poetic. Jesus looked at the bread and said, "This is my body." He was at a dinner where bread was broken as a sign of community. It has been said that the fragmented bread was an image of his fragmented body that would soon be crucified. But we shouldn't lose sight of breaking bread as the sign of brotherhood and sisterhood—the essence of Jesus' teaching. To have a real community, you have to break up as individuals and also come together as a group.

Antoni says that when she first began licking her chocolate self, she was taken by the deconstruction of the image. Something happened to it. It became less real, less a traditional, stuffy bust, a formal representation of herself, and something new and fresh. If we were to understand that incorporating the whole of Jesus in the bread meant appropriating his vision for humanity, then time after time of sacred eating we might be transformed into that vision. We might begin to embody those teachings in our own physical life, in a sense becoming the bread that he blessed and broke.

Sacred Conviviality

On that very day two of them were going to a village called Emmaus about seven miles from Jerusalem. They were discussing everything that had happened. As they talked to each other, Jesus came up and walked along with them, but they didn't recognize him with their eyes.

He said to them, "What are you talking about as you walk?" Looking sad, they paused. Then one of them, Cleopas, said, "Are you the only visitor to Jerusalem who doesn't know what has happened in the past few days?"

"What?" he said.

"Jesus of Nazareth . . ."

*Then, starting with Moses, he explained everything
written in the Scriptures about himself.*

*As they approached the village where they were
headed, Jesus indicated that he was going further. But they
pressed him: "Stay with us. It's almost evening. The day
is almost over." So he went in and stayed with them.*

*When they were sitting at the table, he took bread
and blessed it and broke it and gave it to them. Then their
eyes cleared and they recognized him and he was no longer
invisible to them. They said to each other, "Were not
our hearts burning inside us on the road when he
spoke and opened the Scriptures to us?"*

—LUKE 24:13–19, 27–32

Here we have a warm, intimate example of breaking bread, making the gesture that best summarizes the
Gospel teachings. We find Jesus in an atmosphere of
gentle, complex conviviality. At the miracle of the loaves
and fishes when mere morsels are distributed to a large
crowd, we get a glimpse of Jesus as source of food, real or
metaphorical. At the last supper, the impending torture
and execution colors the convivial nature of the gathering. But at Emmaus the breaking of bread is simple and
straightforward: Jesus is discovered in an atmosphere of
fellowship. We could draw a basic theological theorem
from this scene: the essence of the kingdom is living
together in joy.[30]

There are many possible meanings for the practice
of breaking bread; certainly one of the most obvious is
the fostering of fellowship. The friends share a meal and
symbolically, whether consciously or not, express that

fellowship in sharing pieces of the one loaf of bread. The idea is conviviality and community, the surest signs of the kingdom.

I am suggesting that the very heart of Jesus' teaching and the primary way of realizing his father's kingdom is the gathering of people over food, a gathering that is complicated by various levels of spiritual meaning.

Nothing represents the kingdom more fully than people gathering together, enjoying each other, breaking bread, and discussing issues of greatest importance. At Emmaus Jesus breaks bread, and in that split second his companions recognize him. Then Jesus disappears from their sight, and they are left with the broken bread.

The intimate gathering, meant to evoke the agape of the Gospels, begins with a discussion of significant history, and there follows a congenial meal that includes the symbolic breaking of bread. Conviviality is essential. The students in the story recognize Jesus in the breaking of the bread and the tenor and intensity of their discussions. Breaking bread together, especially with those who are least likely to be part of your community, is not just a symbol but the very reality of the kingdom.

Jesus' vanishing, too, is part of the story. It appears that his physical presence is not the essential ingredient; the bread is. The bread has no single meaning. It is not an allegory, an image standing in for an idea. It is a rich, endlessly fertile image of Jesus' very nature. When he says at the last supper, "Do this to remember me," he is transferring his physical presence from his body to the gesture of sharing and eating bread. The rite of the bread evokes his presence, as it does at Emmaus. It is an instantaneous recall, going hand in hand with the disappearance of the physical phantasm. Bread, not his body, is now the proper physical correlative of his being.

This story of Emmaus is more important for the future of his followers than the one about establishing the *ecclesia*, the church of his followers, with Peter. Maybe Peter was the rock foundation, but the bread is the heart and soul of the community. The community is more important than the leadership, the conviviality more essential than the rules and doctrines. If you worry about your beliefs and if you are anxious about meeting all the requirements of the institution, chances are the very soul of your religion will disappear. Yet all the attractive stories told about Jesus in the Gospels present a man of soul, someone who goes out of his way to show that legalism and moralism are dangerous to the spiritual life.

The Body Transfigured, or Metamorphosis

Six days later, Jesus took Peter, James, and his brother John with him and led them off up a tall mountain. He metamorphosed before them. His face glowed like the sun, and his garments turned as white as light. Suddenly Moses and Elijah appeared to them, speaking to him.

Peter responded by saying to Jesus, "If you would like, I will build three little houses for you, Moses, and Elijah."

While he was speaking, a bright cloud enveloped them and a voice from the mist said, "This is my much-loved and gratifying son. Listen to him."

When the students heard this, they fell face down and were petrified.

*Then Jesus came and touched them
and said, "Stand up. Don't be afraid."*

When they looked, they saw that he was the only one there.

*As they were coming down from the mountain,
Jesus instructed them, "Don't tell anyone about this
vision until I have wakened from among the dead."*

—MATTHEW 17:19

In this mysterious story, Jesus takes three special students with him to a mountain to have a shared mystical vision, in which he is linked with Moses and Elijah. The mountain, the light, and the appearance of Moses all connect this vision to Mount Sinai and the presentation of the Ten Commandments to humankind. Elijah is the great prophet who could raise the dead and who himself was expected to return. But let's focus on what happens to the body in this vision.

The Gospel uses the word *metamorphosis* for the traditional English *transfiguration*. Meta-morph. Change form. Earlier, we studied a key word in the Gospel teaching, *meta-noia*, a shift in understanding. Both words indicate that to be in the kingdom, you need to make a radical change. You have to live in two profoundly connected but distinct realms. In one, you are an ordinary person. In the other, you are, like Jesus metamorphosed, someone who can be present in the past and someone made transparent and translucent. The spark of divinity in you shines through. Your entire being is changed, as the spiritual life, so vivid and concrete, gives you a glow.

Again, Jesus is like a shaman, able to move between worlds and time periods. He takes his students on a vision quest, to a mountain, where they are apart from their friends and colleagues, where they are susceptible to the vision of transformed human existence. Historically, we have tried hard to adapt Jesus' vision to an increasingly modernist world of scientific facts and materialistic measurements. But the Gospels ask for something entirely different, more like Carlos Castaneda's shamanic teacher trying to get him to let go of the assumptions of the limited world in which he lives. Jesus gives his selected students a taste of transformed existence and teaches them the kind of metamorphosis of human life that takes place when you enter the kingdom.

When you finally "get" the teaching of Jesus and begin to live by a new set of rules—love, forgiveness, conviviality, community, healing, and freedom from demonic preoccupations—your clothes don't suddenly become ultra-white and your face blindingly luminous, but you will be, and appear as, transformed. Your presence will have an electric charge. You will be different, and the effect might well be something akin to bright light.

I have known people who have achieved holiness and who I believe represent the rules of the kingdom. You sense in their presence something special and not quite human, or preternaturally human. As many stories of holiness attest, living beyond self-interest gives you the power of healing and a remarkable presence.

When I was a child, many members of my family would visit a holy man living in a monastery a few miles away in the heart of the city. Father Solanus Casey, who is in the process of being made a saint by the Catholic Church, was both ordinary and spiritually incandescent. My father tells the story of visiting him and discussing plumbing, although my father was there to find healing for a member of the family.

Father Solanus lived for others and yet fully enjoyed life. You can live the kingdom today in your world, but you have to learn the difficult lesson of being completely open to the desire of the father, to do the bidding you hear from the core of life rather than satisfy your own small needs.

Metamorphosis or transfiguration is a natural achievement within the scope of any man or woman. It is entirely different from personal power or happiness or success. These things thrill the ego, while metamorphosis sidesteps the ego altogether. It satisfies at a deep level, but in it there is no preoccupation with personal satisfactions. You don't live life as much as life is lived through you. You have the composure and sense of meaning that this other kind of life offers, but you aren't seeking any affirmation that you are all right or in any way better than others.

You may not see the glow of white light that signals metamorphosis, but others will. That is the psychological paradox of the kingdom: your needs are met, but you aren't aware of that fact because your attention is not on them. This is how we might understand the invitation to humility in the Gospels: not as a masochistic, "poor me" sacrifice of self, but as an enlargement of personality to the point where ego concerns fade far into the background. Deep feelings of community and compassion wipe away anxieties about self, and you stand there identified with humanity rather than with your personal goals. You get out of the way. Your soul and spirit shine. People see an almost palpable spirit in you, and they are drawn to it in a way that they could never be attracted to an ego.

Thus the challenge of the Gospel Jesus is not to believe or obey rules or possess the truth. The real challenge is to metamorphose, an ordinary human being manifesting the Jesus nature. You will feel strong resistance against this Jesus transfiguration. It will seem impractical and self-defeating. But these feelings are precisely the price to be paid for entering what is the most fulfilling kind of life.

CHAPTER 8

REINVENTING THE EGO

Spiritual Vision and Human Emotions

*They went off to a place called Gethsemane, and
Jesus said to his students, "Sit here. I'm going to pray."
He took Peter, James, and John with him. He became
deeply troubled and anxious. "My soul is filled with
sorrow, to the point of death," he told them.*

—MARK 14:32–34

At the end of the supper before his execution,
Jesus walks with a few students across the ravine called
Kedron and prays in the garden of Gethsemane.[31] The
Irish writer John Moriarty interprets crossing the stream
as being "Grand Canyon deep in the world's karma."
That is, Jesus goes infinitely deep into the human con-
dition and into human history, as we all must do, and
then goes up toward his crucifixion and resurrection.

While in the garden, on the cusp between his life and death and between his personal life and his life calling, he prays intensely, saying, "My father, if it is possible, let this cup be taken from me. But not what I want, but what you desire."

Jesus is always attuned to his father's wishes, that is, to the source of his life and destiny. Even when faced with betrayal and torture, he can ask to be excused from his fate and at the same time express his willingness to do what needs to be done. It's tempting to notice his faithfulness and then move on, but there is a crucial pattern in this scene in the garden often honored in art and ritual.

Jesus acknowledges his dread and then agrees to the deeper will. In this he models a new kind of ego. You don't surrender completely to the spiritual challenge, but first acknowledge your fears and concerns. Then you express your willingness to participate in your unfolding fate, which has widespread implications. In this, like Jesus, no matter who you are or how insignificant your life may appear, you are both the private person you know so well and a representative of the human race. Even with your weakness and fear, your willingness to embrace your life affects those around you.

A Jesus ego is not centered only on personal choice and responsibility but also rooted in relatedness and always aware of a larger mission. Today it is tempting to numb ourselves against the horrors that are reported in the news every day, to disown our mutual interdependence. But the Jesus way is to feel the despair and, out of the resulting disturbance, make a difference in the world.

As the 15th-century theologian Nicolaus Cusanus said, the whole of human life individualizes in you.[32]

How you react to your challenges affects the whole. You are an active participant, part of the greater community of beings responsible for the unfolding—another Nicolaus word—of life's possibility.[33] To be a person means to have both deep feelings and a connection to a greater community.

You must have friends, as I do, who have discovered this subtle spiritual truth about being engaged in a bigger world. I know people who have gone to jail for social justice and joined the Peace Corps. For years now, my friend Mike has collected used athletic shoes, cleaned them, and sent them to people in need in America and around the world. I have friends in Belgium, Leonard Appel and Marie Milis, who have spent their lives promoting a greater understanding of the spiritual traditions of the world.

All of these people are living the Gospel ideal of an expanded ego, a larger sense of self, and a greater sense of purpose. For myself, my books reach around the world, but I have wanted to be more active in influencing events. I have tried to be more political and international, but nothing so far has taken root. I keep experimenting because I truly believe that this element of the Gospel spirituality is crucial.

Modern philosophy urges us to take responsibility for our actions in a highly personal way. We should try to understand ourselves and know what is happening around us, and then make our informed decision. Through psychoanalysis we should even do our best to understand our unconscious motives. This modern self has few windows onto the transcendent and is therefore trapped in itself, a profound kind of narcissism in which there is no exit to world and community.

But Jesus is not a psychoanalyst. He is keenly aware of a larger context in which his own desires play out. He is Jesus and he is Christ, the man and the "messiah," anointed for a greater mission. He is not an isolated self but the son of the father of life. He never forgets his role as mediator for that profound fathering, and we are invited to follow his example.

The Olive Oil Man

Oil is an important substance in the story of Jesus. The name "Christ" means "anointed" and goes back to the word for olive oil. Jesus is the man of olive oil, the all-important ingredient of cooking and healing. Just as wine is made from the pressing and fermenting of grapes, associated with an image of crushing and a high level of taste and potency, olive oil comes from the pressing of olives and raises both food prepared with it and a person anointed with it to a higher level of potency and spirit. "Christ" means "raised to the level of spirit" or "of new vision." In the chapter on Cana, we saw that the movement from water to wine is an image of metanoia, the shift to a new level of imagination. Anointing with oil is, similarly, the initiation into a new level of being.

I said at the beginning that the secret of the meaning of the Gospels lies in the word *Christ*. It represents the transformation from ordinary, unconscious living to a life on fire with meaning and purpose. It also signifies a deeper level of imagination and reminds us that Jesus was a "divine poet," a spiritual teacher who saw beyond the practical and literal levels of understanding to spiritual poetics, a vision of the deeper meaning of the most ordinary things.

We, too, stand at the midpoint between our deepest thoughts and the call of our destiny. Each of us could add the name "Christ" to our names, indicating the two streams that flow through us—the worldly and the spiritual. People speak of the Buddha nature, but we could also speak of the Christ nature. Once you become aware of your destiny and its relation to the world community, nature included, you are anointed. You have the qualities of the Christ, the one who is marked by the oil of his spiritual vision.

Life wants something of you and has placed you in a historical and social context. Your ego doesn't have to be fully responsible for the whole story but can allow a place for the deeper law that is at work at your core. This reverence for a fatherly law at work in the nature of things is the basis of Jesus' personal morality and the means of fulfilling his life purpose. That profound connection, constant and faithful, is also the source of his power to heal, educate, and face the demonic effectively.

In his agony he prayed intensely and his
sweat fell to the ground like drops of blood.

—LUKE 22:44

The Gospel uses powerful words to describe Jesus' emotional turmoil. He is not an otherworldly superman or a bloodless angel removed from human passion. That is the classic mistake or "heresy," called Docetism, of seeing Jesus only as a rarified spiritual being whose physical body was an illusion. It would be wrong to use Jesus spirituality to avoid the pain and struggle of existence. Jesus goes as deep into suffering as he reaches high in his spirituality. The depth of his emotion gives human grounding to his godlike vision. Both together make him a model of compassion and responsiveness.

The Christ identity means nothing less than feeling fear, dread, distress, worry, concern, compassion, and disillusionment as profoundly as possible and not escaping it in any measure. Only from that bitter depth can you get a glimpse of the bigger plan. You don't go high to escape your disturbing feelings but remain close to your troubling emotions, which become an impetus for an effective spiritual vision.

The Ego and the Father

He said, "Abba, Father, to you everything
is possible. Take this cup away from me.
But not what I wish for but what you want."

—MARK 14:36

Psychologists and spiritual teachers sometimes give the impression that having an ego is more of a problem than a blessing. But an ego is not necessarily the ego of egotism or the self of selfishness. Having an ego essentially means having a sense of subjectivity, a self in the purest sense. It could mean being self-possessed and confident, able to act and accomplish, and capable of relationship.

A sense of self helps organize a world and establish a feeling of agency and capacity. It is of great importance to the whole person, because the ego is the channel and instrument of the more vast and profound soul. A strong sense of self breeds happiness and a feeling of belonging to the world and participating in life.

But an ego is not only a tool for dealing with practical life. It is also a muscle of imagination that is attentive to the inner world and the spiritual realm. It stands in the middle, always a mediator, between visible and invisible life. It serves the soul, the spirit, and the body. It has a Mercury or Hermes quality, the capacity to bring realms together, to be a powerful interface.

On the other hand, when this highly effective ego is lacking, a person usually tries too hard to get it and then struggles with a pseudo-ego, a desperate, elusive attempt to be somebody and to be effective in life. The result is egotism, narcissism, insecurity, domination, and submission—hardly attractive alternatives.

The ego is one complex among many that makes us who we are. It has strong archetypal roots. That is to say, it is an essential ingredient in human life, and the emotions that whirl around it are powerful because they affect our very identity. We properly crave it and struggle with it.

It's interesting to examine the Gospels for signs of Jesus' ego. What is he like as a self? What kind of self does he promote? We have seen that he allows himself to be profoundly disturbed and anxious. This is saying a lot, because ordinarily people do not let themselves fully experience the burden of their lives, and for that reason they don't always know what it is to be a self.

But Jesus understands that a sense of self includes the higher intuitions and inspirations as well. In this regard, he is ever conscious of his "heavenly father" and the demands made of him. But, in order not to be naïve about the father, we need to look again more closely at the nature of a heavenly rather than an earthly father. We have already considered the nature of the father as a heavenly, or Ouranos, spirit. Here, let's think about the father qualities of life itself.

This father aspect is not some simplistic conception of a paternal being in the sky. It is a quality of life, the element that makes of you a story and a personality. It is the procreative factor, a force that can be felt in ordinary situations as generating your existence. Life both mothers and fathers us, and at a time when the role of father has been criticized extensively and that of the mother perhaps understandably overemphasized, it may be necessary to reconsider the importance of this paternal archetype at work in human affairs.

Jesus' term "heavenly father" might be reversed: "fatherly heaven." When you look closely at the nature of things, you can follow science for a long way, but then you come up against moral conflict, the search for meaning, the mysteries of love and connection and failure and redemption. You are now approaching the boundaries of the not-so-human, and this otherworld, which is beyond the limits of the rational and the purely personal, represents the foothills of heaven. There you may sense a paternal quality. You may intuit a spiritual fathering in the background, and you may be inspired to connect to that father in prayer and action.

It might be better to intuit a father quality in the background of your existence than to choose whether or not to believe in a father God offered by formal religion. If you don't have a deeper sense of the paternal actually at work in your life, then your belief will be an abstract experience. You will pray to the Father only because you have been told to do so. But if you glimpse a father spirit in life as you experience it, you will more easily emulate Jesus' intelligent perception of a greater will urging him toward his destiny.

When Jesus honors his heavenly father, as he does continually in the Gospels, he is showing a certain holiness of ego, a sense of self open to the mysteries of existence. Clearly, he doesn't pray to an abstract father principle, but neither does he exhibit the infantilism that people sometimes bring to their idea of the divine father. He completely adopts the role of the father's son, but he doesn't engage in childish religiosity. He honors the father as a profound will deep in the nature of things. Unless you grant the divine father his holiness and mysteriousness, you can't see the intelligence in Jesus' reconstruction of the self.

At Gethsemane, Jesus earnestly wishes to avoid the pain and torment of his approaching conviction and execution, and at the same time he has a stronger wish to honor the desire of the heavenly father. Too often we hear the word *will* used for this clash, but the Greek text speaks of *consent,* which is a richer and more soulful word. Gethsemane is not a battle of wills but a meeting of intentions. Life wants something of us, and that intention runs up against what we want in the narrow confines of the shrunken self.

Jesus hints at a dialectic, a constant conversation between your private hopes and the claims of life on you. This dialogue is the very essence of the religion and the core of Gospel spirituality. At its deepest level, to be religious means to accept your relation to the mysterious purposes life has ordained. Religion is the capacity to consent to what you would not seek but know to be the fulfillment of your destiny.

When I use the word *religion* here, I'm not speaking of an institution, although in the best of worlds a church could serve this purpose. Religion is an attitude of respect for the mysteries that lie beyond our understanding, our control, and our wishes. Religion is a bridge between the mysterious and the known, between what we can accomplish on our own and that which requires help from beyond us.

The Gospels refer to Jesus as both "son of man" and "son of God." It is the nexus of these two identities that constitutes Jesus' religion. It all begins when he stands in the river to be baptized. In the deepest sense, baptism is not just as a formal church ritual but a turning point in life, when you agree to be alive and stand in the streaming of your existence. In effect, you say that you trust this life and give yourself to it. You will not unconsciously follow the crowd and live vicariously. You will be a thoughtful, daring person and an active participant.

The river Jordan and the garden Gethsemane mark the two poles in the arc of Jesus' biography. First he agrees to be a vital participant in the life into which he has been born. Then, later, he confirms this choice in the face of persecution and torment. In both instances he demonstrates his humanity in his humble submission to life and shows his transcendent spirituality by being profoundly connected to the fatherly source of his existence. In his anxiety he can consent to divine, paternal necessity.

Oscar Wilde once said that the Delphic oracle advises, "Know yourself," while Jesus says, "Be yourself."[34] There is a crucial difference between self-understanding and self-realization. Jesus is the principle of life. In everything he says and does he works against the denial and avoidance of life. He embraces it and encourages all to do the same. He immerses himself in both human frailty and human possibility, in both the torment of being a person and the visionary brilliance of being a son of God.

The Garden of Olives

I'd like to make a personal digression here about a recent experience of my own, crossing the Kedron and sweating blood in my garden of olives.

After beginning this book, a new chapter in my life began. I discovered, to my surprise, that I have heart disease. One minute my life was going along with its usual speed and unconsciousness and the next I was dealing with all the implications of my mortality. From my personal point of view, I could well do without this intrusion, but I am already learning many new, transforming lessons as I deal with it. I see firsthand that it takes a spiritual perspective to get beyond the basic position that illness is a problem to be solved. There is a line in Mircea Eliade's diaries where he says that illness is an initiation, a rite of passage, and represents an opportunity to go to a new level in body and spirit.

I have always thought of myself as someone who lives and works from his heart. When I write books and essays, I always try to give them a heart, partly by not hiding in the words and ideas and partly by bringing some warmth and openness to the language. When I lecture, I don't use notes and I try not to give a "canned" presentation. When I sign books for long lines of people, I try to be present to each person and I usually write a brief original message.

Obviously, these are small things compared to the heart needs of the world, and clearly I could go much further toward opening my heart. It is a perfect time for me to be writing about Jesus, who was honored in my Catholic heritage for his "Sacred Heart." And, as I try to show in these pages, he did indeed live and teach with an exceptionally open heart. He could feel deeply and could empathize with all except those who treated others with coldness.

I realize that in many quarters these thoughts could be construed as part of the sentimentality associated with Jesus. But to speak of the heart is not to sentimentalize but to ensoul. There is a toughness and intelligence about living from the heart, and if we interpret the widespread occurrence of heart disease in modern life as a problem of the emotional and relational heart, we can recognize our failure to live with sufficient and sincere compassion.

My heart problems have led me, among many other things, to reconnect with life in two ways. In preparation for a course I am to teach, I came across the powerful African ritual of calling on ancestors and trusting that they are the ones who heal and help sort out life. So I connected to my relatives and friends who have recently died and those who left this plane years ago and even those I never think about—the great-great-grandmothers and great-great-grandfathers and granduncles and grandaunts and far-branching cousins. I brought to mind my daughter's potential children and grandchildren and great-grandchildren, for whom I already feel love.

I also discovered a huge heart-shaped boulder in the thin woods that line our road, and I regularly place my heart against it and feel the granite as part of my existence. In his time of torment, Jesus had his olive trees, his brook of Kedron, and his hill of Gethsemane. I have my New Hampshire heart-rock and the ghost-white paper birches and the crisp, flowing, low-mountain streams. I heard another healer tell of how his powers seem to come from the lines of the land, and I adopted that insight by taking into my deepest imagination my own heart and the particular forms of nature that fill my outward environment and are mirrored in my inward soul.

I see the Jesus-nature in that mammoth rock in front of our house and understand just a bit more of what he meant when he said, "Lift a stone, and I am there." I can't lift that stone literally, but it lifts me when I touch it. Years ago I learned from another student of Jesus, Marsilio Ficino, that special powers lie in objects of nature that resemble other things in color, shape, or even smell. For him, a stone that looks like a heart would have special effectiveness for the human heart.

This kind of spiritual imagination isn't easy to cultivate in modern times, when we are all affected by the demands of science for measurement, reasoning, and evidence. Either we lean toward the modern and are skeptical of far-fetched ideas like those of Ficino or we fall into the silliness of an excessive New Age gullibility unchecked by a critical mind. I try to keep the heart and the mind in dialogue and always aim for intelligence in matters of spirit.

I find that in this time of personal threat it isn't easy to follow the way of Jesus in the garden—entering fully into my fears and my own will and then capitulating to the design life has for me. Is there anything quite as difficult as attuning your desires to those of the life flowing freely through you? To say, "Whatever you want of me, I submit."

My own wish to enjoy the full flow of my life, to be there with my wife and children as they mature, now meets a blockage in a main artery of the heart, where life has failed to flow and where death clearly has an entry. My own desires are clear, but I can only wait and watch for signs of the father's intentions. How difficult it is to pray, "Not my desires, but yours, be fulfilled."

Jesus' students, the Gospel reminds us, used to spend time with him in the garden of olives. Now, at the end, they fail him by falling asleep instead of sharing in his agony. They are confused and in disarray as he is betrayed and arrested. Life begins to fragment, leading soon to the Dionysian dismemberment of the crucifixion.

We all have our olive gardens of despair. The key is to realize that life finds its ground in these moments. It is no time to fall into unconsciousness. Indeed, the garden of despair is a portion of bliss, not to be avoided or discounted.

The Transparent Self

If you love those who love you, what virtue lies in that? Even the morally weak love those who love them. And if you are good to those who are good to you, what virtue lies in that? Even the morally weak do that . . . Love your enemies. Be good to them. Share with them without expecting anything in return. Then your reward will be rich, and you will be sons of the most high. He is kind to the ungrateful and the wicked. Be compassionate, like your father.

—LUKE 6:32–36

The Gospel presents Jesus as a man without guile. He has no personal agenda and is disarmingly forgiving and accepting. When everyone else is judgmental, he is full of understanding. He sides with the victims of oppression rather than with those in power. Yet, he himself doesn't go around with a victim's self-pity. He has the personal power you sense in people who have achieved a level of spiritual maturity.

This, too, is a different kind of self. This aspect of Jesus is very close to the ideal of Taoism, where you lead without arrogance and accomplish much without using force. This paradoxical ideal combines strength and vulnerability. Lao-tzu says:

> The sage has no mind of his own.
> He is aware of the needs of others.
>
> I am good to people who are good.
> I am also good to people who are not good.
> Because Virtue is goodness.
>
> The sage is shy and humble—
> to the world he seems confusing.
> Men look to him and listen.
> He behaves like a little child.[35]

Here we sense a quality in Jesus expounded by mystics—sacred foolishness. There is something foolish and misguided about suggesting such a level of guilelessness. Should you go so far as to be good to those who despise you? Isn't that naïve? Doesn't that insult your intelligence and diminish your judgment? Interestingly, both Lao-tzu and Jesus compare their approach to the behavior of a child.

Some reject Jesus' vision precisely for what appears to be an alarming lack of street smarts. In that case, it might help to recall the idea of the kingdom, where Jesus presents a set of values intended as alternatives to conventional wisdom. The old way simply doesn't work. It results in dominance, aggression, oppression, and violence—in homes and on the international scene. The new way is profoundly unconventional and, as we have seen, demands a basic shift in imagination.

The lack of guile in Jesus is connected to the fact that he is not paranoid. The modern self is afraid of the other. Maybe the other person has something I want or lives in a way that I don't understand. Even contemporary followers of Jesus don't escape paranoia but often fail to honor the spiritual insights of others. They sometimes appear anxiously over-certain about the truth of their convictions, leaving no room for human intellectual frailty and moral development and no room for alternative and challenging points of view.

The unconventionality and paradox in Jesus' teaching comes across forcefully in his prayer among the olive trees, emblems of metanoia. If you love only those who love you, your love isn't very mature. In fact, it is narcissistic. The word *agape* appears over 300 times in the New Testament, such is its importance. In context, it connotes a communal feeling of connection, which Paul spells out as being selfless and which is the opposite of narcissism.

Jesus' words also suggest that the idea is not to create a community of people who like and understand each other, but a different kind of community altogether, one in which people don't understand each other, don't live alike, and are struggling, at best, to love each other.

Be good to your enemies, he says. It is such a radical, unreasonable teaching that people twist his words to avoid it. If you were to follow this injunction, you would definitely find yourself in an alternative reality, in a kingdom significantly different from the world you know and love. It goes against conventional wisdom, the ways of the world, and plain, unrefined passion.

The two weeks that followed the attack on the World Trade Center on September 11, 2001, were intensely quiet. Of course, the generals were planning their counterattacks, but nothing was happening in a world stunned by the barbarism of the atrocity. During those weeks, like so many others, I felt anxious, afraid that further attacks would follow. I feared for my children especially. But I could sense the positive, creative, and hopeful power in that brief interlude when there were no signs of revenge. I thought that America had an opportunity at that moment to truly be a moral leader for the world.

But then the bombs began to drop, and as I write they haven't stopped. America has fallen in the world's view as a moral leader and has lost much of its credibility. The Taoist ideal was ignored and Jesus' appeal not to have enemies was completely overrun.

I think that the Jesus response would have begun with an appreciation for the power of turning the other cheek, not literally to ask for more violence but to resist acting from the unconscious, emotional urge toward revenge. Not to react in typical violent ways would have stunned the world and given America a moral potency unimaginable in any other circumstances. The Jesus way is not the way of knee-jerk, eye-for-an-eye violence; it is a breathtaking refusal to act from pure passion and vengeance.

The very idea of self has to change before the Jesus vision can be adopted. Without being aware of it, we usually assume that the self is something to be defended and thrust in the face of the other. Here, we are told to do the unreasonable and not immediately presume to protect the self. Let your actions go out directly from the heart and not from anxious self-protection.

If you act in this unconventional way, you will be children of the most high, citizens of heaven, and members of the kingdom, and you will be imitating the love of the father for his creatures. This agape is not a purely human love, though it is based in profound emotions of human community. It transcends raw feelings of self-centeredness and therefore takes you outside conventional human wisdom and practice. By loving without expectation, you find yourself in the heavenly kingdom.

In this context, spirituality is not a separate sphere of prayerful action and contemplation but a transformation of ordinary human acts and attitudes. It involves a cleansing of neurotic self-centeredness and the adoption of a completely new set of standards. The agape that Jesus teaches and demonstrates is a spiritually refined form of love. It is not romantic love, nor is it exactly friendship. It is an experience of communal enjoyment of another that doesn't demand conformity or even a return of love. If the love you're thinking of is plain and simple, then it isn't Jesus agape. This kind of loving requires an education in the spirit, a healing of mind and heart, and a true baptism—coming into a new level of being by entering the flowing stream of vitality.

Today many people have a banker's idea of love. If you don't get back as much as you put in, you are being cheated. You need to find someone new to be a friend or lover. But in the context of the Gospels, agape is different. This love doesn't depend on the other's actions. There are no guarantees. The loving is not about you at all. It isn't exactly selfless, because the self is fully involved. But it is a self defined by engagement with others.

This doesn't mean you should suffer abuse at the hands of those you love. As Jesus says more than once, you always have to love yourself in equal measure. This kind of love doesn't proceed from emotional need for security or completion. Agape is not plain emotion; it is a posture toward the world.

As we explore the new sense of self that the Gospels imply, we find ourselves back in the realm of agape. The Gospel ego doesn't operate primarily with mind or will but with the heart. It is openness to experience, to the opportunities and challenges that life offers. It desires an ever-increasing flow of life rather than self-protection. Its way of getting what it needs is to go out of itself.

The Gospel ego is not only altruistic; it is also intimate. Agape can find its way into romantic love and friendship. But we are just beginning to discover and appreciate this kind of agape in the life and teachings of Jesus.

CHAPTER 9

MARY MAGDALEN, WHOM HE LOVED

The Sacred Embrace

Jesus said to her, "Mary." She turned to him and spoke to him in Hebrew: "Rabboni [teacher]," she said. Jesus said, "Don't embrace me. I haven't gone up to the father yet. No, go to my brothers and tell them I am ascending to my father and your father, to my God and your God. Mary Magdalen went to the students and told them the news that she had seen the Lord and he had said these things to her.

—JOHN 20:16–18

In the moving passage quoted above, Mary Magdalen is neither sinner nor servant. She enjoys a place of enormous privilege in the community around Jesus. She is the first to speak to Jesus after the passion of his death and his return, when he is fresh from his ordeal and in a mysterious state, seen now only in vision or in eerie circumstances. It is her role now to tell the other students of Jesus that he has been seen and has said certain crucial things. He is now alive in some way, and a new chapter has begun in the remarkable events surrounding him.

Today, this Mary is the object of intense study and speculation. By now, the average person knows of stories that perhaps she and Jesus were lovers or even husband and wife; that she may have traveled to France and begun a line of Jesus' descendants. Before, she was confused with the prostitute in the Gospels, but now she is made into a saint, perhaps the "beloved disciple" to whom the Gospels never refer by name, and a figure of great importance in the earliest leadership of Jesus' followers.

In this book I have chosen to take seriously many of the noncanonical books, some of which have been discovered rather recently. But I have avoided speculating about historical matters. There is little historical information in the Gospels to go on, and I have no interest in making mountains out of molehills. Still, the figure of this Mary is indeed significant, and without pushing the historical record, I do want to explore the implications of her restoration to prominence based on a close reading of the early documents.

A Sexual Jesus

What is shocking about the new view of Mary Magdalen and Jesus, of course, is the implication that Jesus was not celibate. People who see Jesus in an entirely spiritual light may have trouble considering the possibility that he was a sexual being as well. Yet, as many have said, if you're going to acknowledge Jesus' humanity, you have to include his sexuality.

This doesn't mean that you have to conclude that he wasn't celibate. Everyone has a sexual nature, whether or not he or she acts on it. Celibacy is part of the rhythm of a person's sexuality, and a few choose it as a lifelong commitment.

It would be an error, according to traditional theology, to think of Jesus as pure spirit and therefore as asexual. It is best to picture Jesus as a loving, sexual man who was able to combine close personal attachments with a felt compassion for people he met on his way. His sexuality comes through in his openness of heart, his capacity for intimate relationships, and his love of the good life.

If you still have trouble imagining Jesus as a sexual man, you may have to reflect on what you were taught about him. You may have grown up cherishing the idea that the object of your devotion had nothing to do with the sensuality and sheer physicality of life that you know through your own sexuality. You may want and need a sexless focus for your spirituality. Now you are being asked by many authors to change that point of view. It isn't easy for everyone, and of course, it isn't necessary. As I said, there is precious little information to go on, and you can certainly keep your idea of Jesus as celibate.

Sexual style is an aspect of life that each person develops individually. Traditionally, religion surrounds this process with anxiety and reserve, and the result is often highly neurotic and dangerous. Witness the vast impact of clergy abuse in the Catholic Church. Jesus is unique in many ways, including his sexuality. The Gospels give no indication that he had a wife and children, but they do portray a loving and sensual man. The complexity of his sexuality is a positive aspect of his being and his message.

How you imagine Jesus' sexuality may depend on how you feel about sex. If you think it's contemptible or at least a low part of human nature, you may not want a sexual picture of Jesus. If you see the beauty and full significance of sexuality, you may understand how important it is to allow Jesus his sexuality. Anything less acknowledges his incarnation *except* for sexuality—and that makes no sense.

A heightened awareness of the positive role of Mary Magdalen provides an opportunity to deal with a major problem in all spiritual pursuits: reconciling sexual needs and spiritual ideals. The conflict between sex and spirit, which is detrimental to both, is not limited to the followers of Jesus. All spiritual traditions struggle with the tendency to have a negative opinion of the body and the material world. That negativity easily seeps over into sexuality. In fact, as a psychotherapist, I have the impression that a majority of people raised in religious households have a problem reconciling their sexuality with their spirituality.

So let's not get bogged down in debates about history, whether Jesus and Mary Magdalen were lovers and partners. Since early Gospel-like texts about Jesus offer a more influential role to Mary Magdalen and in rare cases suggest a sexual connection, I would like to consider the positive implications of this union for a contemporary Jesus spirituality. Historically, it is all tentative. Theologically, it is considerably outside the envelope of tradition. Yet it is stimulating to the imagination and offers a possible solution to the serious problem.

A Tantric Gospel

The companion of the Son is Miriam of Magdala.
The Teacher loved her more than all the disciples;
He often kissed her on the mouth . . .

What is the bridal chamber,
If not the place of trust and consciousness
of the embrace? It is an icon of Union.

—GOSPEL OF PHILIP 69, 76 (LELOUP)

The Gospel of Philip, one of the documents found in the Nag Hammadi library in 1945, is a hodgepodge of scenes and teachings, apparently Gnostic in context. It is written in Coptic, an old Egyptian language, and offers the most vivid images of Jesus as a sexual man.

Many passages from the Gospels say clearly that Jesus loved this Mary in a special way. The Gospel of Philip implies that their love was sensual. But Leloup's translation, which is both controversial and disputed, also hints at a kind of sexual spirituality known in other places, as in the Tantric tradition in India, where the marriage bed is "an icon of Union," an image of intense spiritual devotion expressed in sexual imagery.

Sexual expression is not just about communicating emotions or even celebrating a human relationship. It is also a ritual expression for a much deeper union within the self and for the human response to life and to nature. Ordinary sexual expression can convey the closeness we can enjoy with God, with the very source of existence. Allowing for important differences, I might link together the Old Testament Song of Songs, Islamic love poetry, the Tantric paintings and poetry of India, and the Gospel images of Mary Magdalen and Jesus. They all offer a profound spiritual way of understanding sex.

The privileging of Mary Magdalen and the suggestion of a sexual connection between her and Jesus fills a gap that otherwise threatens to ruin the spirituality of the Gospels. What happens to sex if it is not included in the stories and images of the religion? It remains shallow and wholly secular if it lacks an integral connection with spirit. The Gospels, in turn, appear defensive and incomplete, as though sex were something too disgusting to consider positively. The absence of sex also traditionally implies that the woman is a temptation and a threat to purity of heart. The current interest in Mary Magdalen helps restore the depth and symbolic richness of sexuality and femininity to the spiritual life.

We can also understand Mary and Jesus in the light of sexual unions in other religions. It's true that followers of Jesus have claimed superiority for being above sex and in doing so have distanced themselves from paganism. But this purity is shallow and ultimately inhumane. The Catholic Church has paid dearly for its habit of presenting purity to the world while a deep shadow of sexual misbehavior lies beneath the surface. But not only the Catholics: many followers of Jesus show signs of neurosis that comes from the attempt to deny sexuality.[36]

For Westerners, the shocker in Tantra is that sex is a medium for connecting with the divine. For example, one instruction reads: "A man should meditate on his female companion as the embodiment of the goddess's form, until intense practice produces clear, direct vision."[37] This meditation can be done either during sex (*maithuna*) or as a visualization. Tantric practitioners can also contemplate images of the male and female together in embrace. In Tantra, sex is in the service of spirituality.

Sex takes you out of yourself, and, if done in certain ways, gets the ego out of the way. You are then in a position to perceive the divine within yourself and in another. The intense passions aroused by a partner morph into the desire for union with God. Your partner is a medium for deep spiritual contact.

Tantric sex is serious, spiritual sensuality shaped into religious devotion. It is not about the ego or even human relationships, but about God. Here you find the spiritual core of your identity. Why do all those figures surround Hindu temples such as Khajuraho in all forms of dance and lovemaking, except to show how sexuality holds the secret of the relationship between human and divine?

It is a tragedy that Christianity has developed without a similar appreciation for the spirituality of sex. Because of its anti-sexual attitude, countless lives have been thrown into confusion and battered by guilt and self-denial. Worse, the suppression of sexuality, even for the highest of motives, eventually leads to aggression against self or others. Sexually repressed people become condemning, rigid, and self-righteous and blindly act out the aggression rooted in the suppression of Eros.

So it is of great importance that finally we are finding a way out of repression through the striking figure of Mary Magdalen. She is once again a true saint, not because she repented of her sexual sins—that story reflects the very repression we are discussing—but because she is seen to be especially close to Jesus, even his lover. She is his chosen one and, for his followers, a beloved leader.

Over the centuries, followers of Jesus have allowed devotion to the other exalted woman in his life, his mother, Mary. Jung thought that the dogma of the Church celebrating Mary's "assumption" into heaven, taking her place in the highest domain, was an extremely important spiritual and psychological development. It allowed Jesus spirituality to be joined by an anima figure, a representative of soul. Recent serious studies of Mary Magdalen serve a similar purpose: they invite a different sort of anima figure, the lover, to be included in the spirituality of Jesus. In the history of Gospel spirituality, this may be the most important development.

For too long, followers of Jesus have been shackled with a sordid view of sex. The new estimation of Mary Magdalen promises a view of sex as an avenue to the divine. This is sex in service of the spirit and soul. This is sex in the kingdom.

The Sacred Prostitute

Peter said to Mary, "Sister, we know the savior loved you more than any other woman. Tell us the words of the savior that you remember, which you know but we do not, because we have not heard them." Mary answered and said, "What is hidden from you I shall reveal to you."

—GOSPEL OF MARY 20 (MEYER)

Contemporary scholars go to great pains to remind us that in the Gospels, Mary Magdalen is not a prostitute. That is another person from another story. Nor is she the woman with the alabaster jar who anoints Jesus' feet with her hair. But Mary *is* described as a woman who has had seven demons cast out of her. Maybe that is why she has so easily been confused with the prostitute. The first thing many people think of when they hear the word *demonic* is sex.

It's important to get our images right, to sort out these women and be clear about who Mary Magdalen was. At the same time, it is interesting to note how the imagination has clung to the idea that Mary was a prostitute. Some like the sentimental idea of Jesus reforming a woman of the streets. But I think that deep down we are also drawn to the notion of the dark side of the Jesus story, the repressed sexuality, coming onto the scene. It is somehow satisfying that Mary Magdalen is part of the picture. How else can we understand the near-hysterical interest in Jesus and this Mary in recent years? Or the intense interest shown in Mary in paintings and sculptures?

The continuing success of books about Mary Magdalen shows how anxiously we look for a way to deal with sexuality. She is like Venus to the Romans and Aphrodite to the Greeks: a powerful image of sexuality that requires our compliance at the cost of at least a portion of our innocence. She darkens the Gospel story, and that darkness is precious, saving the spiritual life from the sentimentality or excessive innocence that is always a temptation.

The image of Jesus and Mary Magdalen loving each other, kissing each other, goes deep. It offers an entirely different way of imagining spiritual dedication. It brings sex into the equation of being fully human and fully spiritual. It helps bridge the gender gap in spiritual matters. It helps us appreciate masculinity and femininity and intimate contact between the two.

The various Gospels offer a complicated and contradictory picture of who Jesus was and is. On one hand, they clearly provide a portrait of a celibate but loving man; on the other hand, they suggest that Jesus had a lover and confidante in Mary Magdalen. We can't fully reconcile these different views, but we might benefit from remaining in the tension between the two. Somewhere between celibacy and marital sex lies an image of how to be a spiritual person while expressing your own unique sexuality.

The Goddess of Sexual Embrace

When Eve was in Adam, there was no death. When she was separated from him, death came. If she enters into him again and he embraces her, death will cease to be.

—GOSPEL OF PHILIP 52 (MEYER)

If Dionysus shines through in Jesus the vine and maker of wine, then Aphrodite shines through in Mary Magdalen. She and Jesus together represent what religion scholars and depth psychologists speak of as *hieros gamos,* the great mythic union of the masculine and feminine that is so prominent in many religions.

For the ancient Greeks, Zeus and Hera were ideal types of human unions and the source of all vitality. The Greeks said the lovemaking of this divine couple seeded the universe with vitality and meaning. In India, the union of god and goddess, such as that of Vishnu and Lakshmi, unleashes the vital power of life in its creative and destructive aspects. In the ancient Near East, the union of Marduk and Ishtar has similar life-sustaining power.

In spiritual literature, sexuality and marriage represent the union of all opposites. Life cannot go on freely when opposites are split apart—mind and body, masculine and feminine, soul and spirit, joy and sadness, strength and vulnerability. The women of the Gospels are of great importance in overcoming the split when Jesus and his spirit father completely dominate the spiritual realm.

Mary Magdalen is essential not only for healing the split of masculine and feminine, but also for sustaining the central Gospel idea that a woman from whom seven demons had been expelled could be the closest and most informed figure among Jesus' students. For us it means that it is not in spite of our past mistakes and moral failings, but precisely because of them, that we can be part of the spiritual community Jesus called "the kingdom." We don't have to reform ourselves as much as we have to own and acknowledge our weakness and ignorance. Emptying ourselves of a sense of worthiness and specialness, we are prepared to be in this world with an open heart, full compassion, and acceptance.

CHAPTER 10

COME OUT, LAZARUS

An Invitation to Life

*As they were coming down the mountain, Jesus told them
not to say anything about what they had seen until the
son of man had risen from the dead. They kept this idea to
themselves, discussing what "rising from the dead" could be.*

—MARK 9:9–10

Jesus the Shaman

The story of Lazarus coming out of his tomb trailing
his burial wrappings echoes through history. But usually
it is told in the old defensive context of proving Jesus'
powers over nature, with a hint at the tale of his own
resurrection. Lazarus' connection to the kingdom is lost,
but one way to go deeper is to reflect further on the shamanic qualities of Jesus and his mission.

As a go-between for two worlds, the heavenly realm of his father and the earthly domain of his life and work, Jesus, as we have seen, is much like a shaman. A shaman is a man or woman with a special calling to live in two realities at once—the ordinary world we all know well and a deeper, higher reality, both transcendent and profoundly interior, where everything has a spiritual meaning. The shaman sometimes carries a ladder to symbolize the comings and goings between these worlds, and the drum, one of the tools of his trade, may have markings that show the two worlds within a single circle. With his visionary ability to see the spiritual nature of an illness and perceive deep stories hidden within events, a shaman heals and advises his people.

A shaman is schooled in entering strange in-between worlds of imagination. He is a healer and a teacher, a guide of souls. He speaks as though this ordinary world has a richer, hidden dimension. Through music, trance, and prayer he finds his way into areas of inner space that most people are never aware of. He may call this deep interiority the otherworld or the land of the ancestors. He could call it the kingdom of heaven.

The shaman speaks in poetic language, the only way to describe what he sees on the other plane. He may use metaphor, parable, image, story, song, dance, masks, costumes, and props. He leads rituals, heals spiritually, and serves as the messenger to his community from the otherworld.

Jesus' role of go-between, connecting his students to his father, is central to his work. Yet, for all the devotion given in formal religion to God the Father, generally people don't live their lives with the same shamanic participation in the alternate reality. They pray, "Our

Father, who art in Heaven," but they think of heaven as approachable only through death. The shaman travels to "heaven" today, not after death, and knows the realm of spirit as well as he knows the physical world.

Today we tend to rationalize religion, turning it into a philosophy and moral code. We are not visionaries and seers, and we don't aspire to be shamans. But the spirituality Jesus models includes transfigurations and visitations from the heavens. The Gospels tell of these breakthroughs of the sacred and show Jesus to be at home, as any shaman would be, in each.

We have naïve and literal versions of such breakthroughs. As recently as 2008, people in Springfield, Massachusetts, saw a visitation from the Virgin Mary in mineral deposits on a plate-glass window in a doctor's office. At least the spiritual imagination is still at work. But our spirituality could deepen if we could appreciate a shamanic element in Jesus, an ability to live in two worlds and to connect the two.

When he is standing in the river being baptized, he hears his father and sees a bird-spirit in the air above him. Later, for the benefit of his students, he metamorphoses. He tells his friends that they can unite with him through the medium of bread and wine. He heals by touch and word. One would expect his students to do similarly, given that he told his original class to go out and do these things. But today, because of our cramped modern views about what is possible, along with formal religion's emphasis on belief and morality, the shamanic aspect is lost.

A shaman isn't concerned about worshiping the father or adoring any spiritual figure that appears to him—and many do appear. His focus is not on belief and adoration but on obedience, honoring the visions by taking them seriously.

At its root, the word *obedience* means to listen. The shaman listens closely to the word of the spiritual figure and does what is indicated. In the inspiring Sufi story of Majud, an angel appears and tells him to jump into the river. Majud doesn't get caught up in theological arguments about who or what the angel could be; nor does he fall down in worship. He simply jumps in the river. He enters life wholeheartedly.

Similarly, Jesus never asks to be adored or even revered. He recommends a life in tune with the father's purposes. As we have seen, the word used for "will" in the Lord's Prayer—"Thy will be done"—suggests intention and pleasure, not moral demand. The point is not to obey the father as though he were a tyrant or even simply an authority but to fulfill his wishes for the human race. I prefer to translate that passage as "Your wishes be fulfilled" or even "Your wishes for me or for us be fulfilled."

When exceptional people, like shamans, are in touch with the deeper and higher reality, they often find themselves directed to do certain things that may not make sense but seem to serve a hidden, beneficial purpose. An African woman hears a call in the middle of the night to be a healer, and she gets up out of bed and walks immediately to a teacher. This willingness to comply with a greater, mysterious instruction is a sign of her readiness to be a healer.

The same is true of anyone wishing to be a student of Jesus: he has to look for signs of the alternate reality, the kingdom, and be willing to enter it. There he will be able to heal and be healed. There, if he has truly penetrated the other domain, he will live in a world full of powerful imagery and uncanny happenings, all for the advancement of the peaceful, equitable kingdom.

Levels of Vitality

Still today, Jesus' teachings address the crude mechanistic thought that dominates every aspect of modern culture. They propose to wake society from the dumb sleep of materialism and self-absorption. Again and again in the Gospels, he challenges simplistic belief and moralism, which are aspects of the materialism of our age. They are, in the perceptive phrase of the spiritual teacher Chögyam Trungpa, signs of "spiritual materialism."

Trungpa begins his book with an observation that cuts to the center of Jesus' teaching. Of spirituality in general he says, "The teachings are treated as an external thing, external to 'me,' a philosophy which we try to imitate . . . We go through the motions, make the appropriate gestures, but we really do not want to sacrifice any part of our way of life. We become skillful actors, and while playing deaf and dumb to the real meaning of the teachings, we find some comfort in pretending to follow the path."[38]

This is not so much a harsh criticism as a thoughtful warning to students of spirituality not to be complacent in mere attachment to a spiritual path. Just as we madly pursue facts and the control of nature, we tend to treat the mysteries of spirituality and religion as though they were also facts. We don't go deep into them. With respect to Jesus, we ask factually whether he worked wonders or was God or rose physically from death. We may miss the challenge in his teachings to live a different way of life, to take our ideals seriously, and to live the Gospel ideals radically: being a healer, responding to the world community, loving those who are different and who think differently.

Anyone who drinks this water will be thirsty at another time. But anyone who drinks the water I give him will never be thirsty again. The water I give him will be a spring in him, water flowing into eternal life.

—JOHN 4:13–14

Life is like water—vast, surging, and filled with beings of all kinds. To enter the kingdom, you have to be born deep into this fluidity, this teeming nature of life. Jesus stands in the river, an image for life's full, watery nature, and allows the water from that river to flow over him.

Heraclitus spoke of the river aspect of reality. "All things flow," he said. *"Panta rhei." Rhei* is the root of our word *river*. A river flows and gives us an image for how life flows. Heraclitus also said, "You can't step twice into the same river." Nor can you step twice into the same quality of life. It has moved on. The flowing river is a lesson in life: You can't stop it. You can't repeat it. You have to live knowing that it is in constant transformation.

Jesus stepped into that rivering life at the beginning of his career. As we have already seen, at that moment his father appeared in the heavens and said, "This is my son, who is pleasing to me." God the father approves of this action, standing in the flow of life, indicating that being fully alive is identical with being spiritual.

In the religious imagination of India, the Ganges River is the milk of cows and therefore the source of life.

In Paradise, in Genesis, four rivers flow from the garden and water the earth with vitality. In the Book of Revelations there is a life-giving river:

> Then the angel showed me the river of the water of life, bright as crystal, flowing from the throne of God and of the Lamb through the middle of the street of the city. On either side of the river is the tree of life with its twelve kinds of fruit, producing its fruit each month; and the leaves of the tree are for the healing of the nations.
>
> —REVELATIONS 22:12

We have already noted the river of Majud, into which the trusting man leaps at the mere word of an angel. James Joyce begins and ends *Finnegans Wake* with the word *riverrun,* keeping his mythic summary of human existence in eternal rotation. In Hermann Hesse's novel, Siddhartha finds the secret of life at the river.

This relation to the river is the secret of the spiritual life. In this sense, baptism is not limited to any particular religious tradition. It is a requirement for any turn from materialism to spirituality, from unconsciousness to a deep imagination. We can all find the flow, the soul water, the *aqua permanens* of the alchemist, in ourselves. Entering that "water" is our baptism. The flow of life is always the Jordan River.

To be baptized is to discover ritually that life flows. This lesson may appear trite, but it is basic. People live as though life should be static, staying in one place. We think that of marriage, relationships, work, ideas, and values. We try to keep them firm and stable, but life keeps moving. The question is whether you move with the flowing of life or insist on the security you find in stability and control.

Honoring the flow of life is an aspect of being spiritual, and that is why baptism is essential in religions. And it is a short step toward honoring the source of that flow, which Jesus refers to as "my father."

Encased in our modernist world, we are Nicodemus asking how it is possible for an old person to squeeze back into the womb and be born again. We repeat that question whenever we ask how spiritual things work and when we try to explain the spiritual in terms of the factual. Those sorts of questions indicate that we have not left the materialistic viewpoint. As Trungpa says, we may sincerely want to live on a spiritual plane, but we resist making the shift. Like the wealthy young man in the Gospels, to whom Jesus says he would have to give up his wealth to enter the kingdom, we are sad to give up unconsciousness. The wealth Jesus speaks of may not be literal money, although, as we have seen, money can be an obstacle. The wealth we hang on to may be the comfort of not thinking things through and acting on our perceptions.

Whatever your background, you can borrow language from other spiritual traditions. You don't have to be Buddhist to work out the Eightfold Path in your life. You don't have to be Christian to see the importance of baptism. And you don't have to be naïve to see the possibility of resurrection—those who are soul-dead coming back to life.

Now, with some appreciation for spiritual birth, we might be ready to look at Lazarus as he walks smelly and stiff out of his tomb. What are we to make of this miracle, this impossibility? Is Jesus the shaman at work again transforming the world?

Come Out of Your Tomb

*Once again profoundly moved, Jesus approached
the grave. It was a cave with a stone leaning
on it. "Remove the stone," Jesus said.*

*"But Lord," the dead man's sister Martha said,
"it's been four days now. It smells."*

*Jesus said to her, "Didn't I tell you that if
you trusted, you would see the glory of God?"*

*They removed the stone and Jesus raised his eyes and
said, "Father, thank you for listening to me. I know that
you always hear me. I said this for the people gathered
here. Now maybe they'll believe that you sent me."*

After he had said this, Jesus called out, "Come here!"

The dead man came out.

—John 11:38–44

As we have seen, in John, the special things Jesus
does to define himself and describe the kingdom are not
called miracles or wonders but signs—omens, traces,
symbols, images. John tells the story of the blind man
being cured, and then he goes on to describe those who
are blind to meaning in their lives. The miracle isn't
proof that Jesus is a kind of superman; it's a sign to be
read in relation to the teaching about the kingdom.

The Lazarus story, similarly, is a lesson about coming
to life. Some readers see echoes of the Egyptian tale of
Osiris, who dies and comes back to life. Some see it as a

foretelling of Jesus' own death and resurrection. These resonances take nothing away from the story in John, which tells of deep feeling and friendship. They add dimension to the Gospel story and help us see it as an archetypal image that says something about the human condition. The teachings of Jesus tell how to come to life, how to be born in the spirit, and how to resurrect.

The word used for dead, *nekron,* doesn't always refer to actual death but to a state of soul. The prodigal son didn't actually die, but he did lose his soul until he finally came to his senses. It is this kind of death that the "parable" of Lazarus also describes.

In William Blake's words: "May God us keep from single vision and Newton's sleep."[39]

The teaching is all about new and fuller vitality, about waking up to the fact that we have a soul that makes us human and allows us to live and love. As we'll see in detail at the end of this book, Jesus' teaching is all aimed at the resurrection of life in its fullness. Lazarus is the archetype of coming to life after being dead, and his story is about breathing the fresh air of the kingdom instead of the smelly atmosphere of deadly materialism.

Lazarus is everyman. Like him, we are all called to two levels of life: a physical life and a life of spirit and soul. But the life in us can recede and eventually disappear. It can be lost to depression and disillusionment, and it can fade away in materialistic and egotistic pursuits.

Our culture is now enduring a long, gradual descent into a materialistic stupor. In India it is said that we are in the Kali Yuga, a period of decay and loss of humaneness. Both the fact and the threat of war are everywhere, disturbing people across the globe and creating a massive depression, worry about safety, and despair for the happiness of children and young people. Nuclear threat still hangs over us, even after the end of the Cold War. Lazarus is our myth and our condition.

You can imagine Jesus, completely given to the work of wakening and enlivening humanity through a philosophy of love, being profoundly disturbed by our current situation, just as he is by news of his friend's death. The Greek word used in the Gospel to describe Jesus' torment is *embrimomenos*. Notice the little word in the larger one: *em-brimo-menos*. In classical literature, *brimo* is a descriptive name for the goddesses of death, including both Persephone and Hecate, used particularly in relation to the great mystery-ritual of Eleusis. In this highly revered rite, neophytes learned the spiritual lesson of death and resurrection. It was a ritual of hope, culminating in the symbolic birth of a child with the name Brimos. Brimos is Lazarus, and both are us when we come back to life. The Gospels don't make the world better immediately, but they give us a way and some hope.

These associations might help us appreciate the depth and extent of Jesus' sorrow in the story of Lazarus and the great theme of death and resurrection that lies within the tale of two friends. Like all the other Gospel stories, this one builds on the theme of kingdom and the law of agape. It is from love that Jesus brings new life out of death and despair.

Again, it is the task of the student of Jesus to do what he did: Where you find death, you bring forth life. Where there is sadness and depression due to loss of soul, you waken the soul and bring it out of its tomb. In the most ordinary of circumstances, this kind of awakening is experienced as truly miraculous.

I've seen it in therapy. A man or woman has had no life and sees no future, but gradually, with tender care for a fragile soul, new life stirs. I have many memories from my practice of people who were soul-dead coming to life and finding unexpected ways to rejoin community. The secret in each case was love, agape, all of us learning to love the soul, love our fate, and love each other. These were not sentimental cases. It was all difficult work. But when you see life restored in an individual, hope stirs that the world could be revived, if only we could find our way.

Once you shed the idea that a miracle is a work that contradicts natural law and come to see it as achieving what seemed to be impossible, then a story like that of Lazarus takes on new levels of meaning. It is no longer a tale about a corpse emerging zombie-like from its tomb. It's about everyone coming to life in this concrete world and in our own time.

The archetypal tale of Lazarus could be the most important, the central, the defining story of the Gospels. But I'm aware that each time we take one of the stories to its depth, I say the same thing. All the stories point to the same idea. Jesus is revealing a truth that everyone knows but forgets or sets aside: if the world could live by the principle of love, it would find its healing and would come to life.

CHAPTER 11

THE JOYS
OF EARTHLY
EXISTENCE

The Sensuality of the Gospels

*When John the Baptist came, he didn't eat bread
or drink wine, and you said he has a demon.
When the son of man comes he eats and drinks,
and you say that this man who eats and drinks
wine is a friend of tax collectors and wrongdoers.*

—LUKE 7:33–34

A certain kind of worldliness—a crazed pursuit of
money and power and an emphasis on self at the expense
of others—is incompatible with the Jesus domain, but
another approach to worldliness is essential. The Gospels portray Jesus enjoying food and social gatherings,
refusing to condemn people for their sexuality and work
ethic, and in several noncanonical texts he laughs with
his students, obviously enjoying his friendships.

Jesus is a complex figure, a man of contradictions, and not, as he is often presented, one-dimensional. He is very earthy and very spiritual, and these dimensions of his personality and message overlap.

The religious people around him, like many today, took a negative and moralistic attitude toward human pleasures. But in the passage above, Jesus contrasts himself with John the Baptist, who was an ascetic. John didn't eat bread or drink wine, but Jesus does. His critics complain that he enjoys the company of the despised and corrupt tax collectors and criminals and falls short of the spiritual perfection expected of him.

This side of Jesus' character, his affirmation of life's simple pleasures, is of great importance to his teachings. In an earlier chapter I made the case that Jesus was an Epicurean, someone who understood the role of moderate and deep pleasures. Today the word Epicurean usually refers to people who place too much emphasis on fancy food and excessive drinking. But Epicurus the philosopher taught the value of moderation, even though he advocated deep and lasting pleasures.

Epicurus taught his philosophy in a garden at his home, and his community was made up of a wide variety of people, including courtesans. In this he was like Jesus. He valued the simple pleasures, like friendship, which, over the centuries, he and his followers placed among their highest values. Food and fellowship were also important, aimed at a tranquility of soul.

Religious people often split sensuality from spirituality, assuming that the only choice is to be either an ascetic or a hedonist. But the teaching of Epicurus lies in the middle between these extremes. Jesus, too, was neither ascetic nor hedonistic. He was earthy and sublime.

He apparently enjoyed eating—there are many positive references to food in the Gospels—and he drank wine. But the Gospels show him living a simple life, enjoying his friends and rejecting wealth as a preoccupation.

We have a tendency to think of food the way scientists and nutritionists do: as part of the necessary chemistry of keeping the body alive and healthy. But food is also important for the soul. Why else have festive family dinners or lunch with a close friend or a romantic dinner in a special restaurant? You can get the chemicals no matter where you eat, but your soul may need ethnic food, a romantic atmosphere, or a meal full of memories. Jesus accepted Jewish and pagan traditions in which food was part of a spiritual ritual and the means of gathering community.

Mysteriously, food helps people talk and celebrate. This is the kind of food Jesus and Epicurus honor as being essential to the life of soul and spirit. In both philosophies, food and friendship go together.

In another story, a Pharisee asked Jesus to eat with him, and so Jesus went into his house and sat at the table. A woman who had a bad reputation in town heard that he was having dinner at the home of the Pharisee and brought an alabaster jar full of oil. As she knelt behind him at his feet, her tears began to fall, wetting his feet. She wiped them with her hair, kissed them, and anointed them with the oil. The Pharisee host said to himself, "If this man were a prophet, he would know what kind of woman is touching him, that she is wicked." The Gospel picks up the story:

> Jesus said to him, "Simon, I want to tell you something."

He said, "Teacher, speak to me."

"Two men owed money to a lender. One owed five hundred dollars, the other fifty. Neither could afford to pay him, so he canceled both their debts. Now, which of them do you think will love him more?"

Simon replied, "I suppose the one who was freed of the larger debt."

Turning toward the woman, he said to Simon, "Do you see this woman? When I came into your house, you didn't offer me water for my feet, but she wet my feet with her tears and dried them with her hair. You didn't kiss me, but this woman hasn't stopped kissing my feet since I arrived. You didn't offer me oil for my head, but she has poured oil on my feet.

"I'm telling you, because she has so much love, her many acts of wickedness are forgiven. Whoever has found forgiveness for something small doesn't love as much."

Then Jesus told her, "Your bad behavior is forgiven."

—Luke 7:36–48

This is a beautiful story of forgiveness, and it presses, yet again, the theme of metanoia—the transformation in a person who needs it most. But it also shows how Jesus appreciates a degree of sensuality and physical care. Washing, oil, a kiss of greeting—Jesus affirms these simple, sensual acts of kindness and civility, thus incorporating them into his overall philosophy. Excessive purity, moralistic judgment, and abstemiousness have no place there.

A Greek of the time might have noticed that the woman with the alabaster jar represents the sphere of life looked after by the goddess Aphrodite. Sexuality, sensuality, affection, aromatherapy—these are all within the domain of the goddess. Yet, as we saw, the spirituality of this goddess has been a scandal to many followers of Jesus over the centuries. Many people see a strong opposition between the sensuality and pleasure associated with her and the intense spirituality of Jesus. But the Gospel doesn't make this division. In fact, in this key tale, Jesus shows himself clearly on the side of moderate sensual delight.

In an inspired piece of Romantic theology in his letter from prison, *De Profundis*, Oscar Wilde comments on this passage about the woman with the jar and on Jesus' reaction: "If the only thing he had ever said had been 'Her sins are forgiven her because she loved much,' it would have been worthwhile dying to have said it."[40]

It makes all the difference to the spiritual life to give equal attention to the simple joys of daily interaction and to ordinary physical delights. The body is as important in the kingdom as the spirit. Indeed, any spirituality that neglects the body is for that reason off-center and neurotic. Jesus doesn't compensate for this tendency, as some would, by going too far with sensuality. That is not his nature. But neither does he repress it. He is able to live the tensions and contradictions of spirituality and sensuality. He can be completely absorbed in contemplation with his spiritual father and then eat and dance with his friends.[41]

There is nothing clearer in the Gospels: anyone who has made mistakes in a sexual way and has now changed his mind is forgiven for those missteps and indeed ranks high in the kingdom. You don't hear anything about the virtuous, who have never risked overstepping the mark, finding their way into the community of bliss.

This equation, so central to the Gospel teaching, is a great mystery. Somehow, by getting through our sexual confusion and acting-out, we are better prepared than others to be part of the new way of life the Gospel calls "the kingdom." Could it be that by living life to the fullest, making mistakes along the way, we are ready to appreciate the different kind of life the Gospel represents, a life of radical communal love and forgiveness? If we have not risked and have not made mistakes, we don't know firsthand the experience of forgiveness, and without that experience we remain in the vestibule of the kingdom.

This is a subtle point: many would no doubt assume that to be religious you have to do your best to be good and especially keep your sexuality in check. In fact, religion often rewards and admires sexual purity. As a result, many people repress their sexuality because of religion and sometimes feel righteous for doing so. Eventually, though, some reassess their attitude of repression and turn against religion because of it.

Sex is a powerful passion that can be difficult to weave into an ordered life. Some people deal with the problem by living two lives—a surface life of apparent virtue and normalcy and a hidden life of experimentation and exploration. Others, perhaps the majority, try to be moderately virtuous and fail in ordinary ways. In light of the Gospels, those failures are precious because they can fuel a deep change of heart whereby sexuality becomes the basis for communal love.

Many people seem to have the impression that the repression of sensuality is the very meaning of virtue.

But Jesus doesn't model this kind of purity. Like Epicurus, he acknowledges the strength of human passion and the role of desire and pleasure. He connects the two streams of spirit and body, allowing one to condition the other.

The history of Christianity is full of anti-sexual rhetoric and condemnations and punishments. Millions of Christians have suffered the joylessness and truncated relationships caused by a negative attitude toward sexuality. This entire history, lingering into the present, goes against the spirit of the Gospels. One wonders how such a clear pro-sex Gospel teaching could have become so lost and twisted.

In therapy sessions over the years, many people have presented to me their stories of sexual frustration. They were brought up in religion to have a negative and withholding attitude toward sex. In many cases, their marriages suffered as a result. But there is nothing in the Gospels to warrant an anti-erotic approach to life, nothing that says that sex is wrong or evil. The repression came from somewhere else, some other influence on religion that admires repression and judges a sense of virtue as being more "spiritual" than sexual experience.

There was a gathering of Simon Peter,
Thomas Didymus, Nathaniel from Cana in Galilee,
the sons of Zebedee, and two other students.

Simon Peter said, "I'm going to do some fishing."

They said, "We'll come along."
So they went and got in the boat.
But that night they didn't catch anything.

At dawn, Jesus was standing on the beach,
but the students didn't know it was him.

Jesus said to them, "Young people,
haven't you caught anything?"

"No," they said.

He said, "You'll find some if you toss
your net out on the right side of the boat."

They tossed it, and there were now so many
fish in the net that they couldn't haul it in.

The beloved disciple said to Peter, "It's the Lord!"

When Simon Peter heard that it was the Lord, he put on his
clothes—he was almost naked—and jumped in the water.

The others followed in the boat, pulling the net
full of fish. They were only a hundred yards from shore.
When they reached land, they saw a fire and burning
coals. There were fish on it and some bread.

Jesus said to them, "Bring some of
the fish you have caught over here."

Simon Peter climbed onto the boat and dragged
the net ashore. It was teeming with large fish, one
hundred fifty-three of them, and yet the net didn't tear.
Jesus said to them, "Come here and have breakfast."

None of them had the courage to ask,
"Who are you?" They knew it was the Lord.

Jesus approached, took the bread and
gave it to them, and the fish, too.

—JOHN 21:2–13

Yet another charming story, and here, too, Jesus gives his attention to food and to feeding his friends. Here he is the chef, cooking the fish and heating bread on an open fire. The dialogue is not heavy theology, but banter about fishing and eating. Of course, a miracle, the coinage of the Jesus way of life, is happening, too.

But what about the miracle? Remember that the story is told in the John community. There, a miracle is a sign: not factual proof that Jesus is a superman, a wonder-worker, but a sign of what an ordinary human action means in the kingdom.

His students are fishing on the wrong side of the boat. They're doing the proper thing, but they're doing it in the wrong way or in the wrong place. He corrects them, and suddenly they are overwhelmed with fish. It is exactly the same in the kingdom. Any ordinary thing you do with attention to the kingdom will suddenly reap extraordinary riches. It will have touched your soul and spirit and have great meaning to you. The only catch is that you have to know on which side of the boat to cast your net. On one side a life that is familiar and predictable, typically practical and self-interested; on the other side, the kingdom, rich and bountiful but different.

The men caught 153 fish. What could that number mean? It seems absurd to mention such a specific number in the context of a net bursting with fish. David Fideler, an expert in religious symbolism, offers many implications. He says that 153 translates visually and geometrically into the form of a net and is related to the Greek god Apollo and the philosopher Pythagoras, who, according to a story, accurately gave the number of fish caught in a large net. The number also refers to the whole of the cosmos.[42] It also happens to be the number you arrive at when you add the series of numbers from 1 to 17. And it is said that, at the time of Jesus, there were believed to be 153 species of fish.

From all these associations, 153 is clearly a meaningful and symbolic number, generally representing totality. When Jesus' followers fish properly, on the side of life that Jesus knows and represents, they take in all fish. In another context, Jesus had told them he will teach them how to catch people, not only fish. Perhaps this net shows that all people are candidates for the kingdom, all 153 varieties of us.

If you have been living with deep anxiety about yourself, about being somebody, or about having wealth and power, you have been fishing from the wrong side of the boat. This is the key: Jesus consistently talks about an alternative way of being. The usual logic doesn't work. You forgive, you do what is healing, and you deal with the demonic when you come face to face with it. You even disregard the laws of nature, as far as you are able, to accomplish the mission of the kingdom, which is to create an agapic, loving community that excludes no one. The Gospels couldn't be clearer on these points.

Many people seem to think that keeping themselves sexually pure is the most important item in following the teachings of Jesus. But the accent in his teaching is entirely different. He is more worried about wealth than sex, and he is forgiving rather than judgmental. This issue cuts right to the core of Jesus' philosophy: wrapping yourself in virtue or obeying the rules to the letter doesn't get you into the kingdom. Those nets are on the wrong side of the boat. Jesus is closer to the Buddha, whose principal teaching of compassion (*karuna*) is almost indistinguishable from Jesus' teaching of outgoing love (*agape*).

Jesus says clearly that you should love yourself and your neighbor, as though it were the same love. If you think of Jesus as the founder of a religion, you may think that this love should be abstract and bodiless. It should even be free of the needs of the soul for friendship and interpersonal warmth. But if you understand that Jesus was promoting a way of life that is both highly spiritual and earthy, you can allow your love to be physical, sensual, and in some deep way sexual.

Having good friends, treating people well, operating in every instance from a rule of love rather than judgment—this is the soul of the Gospels. Living from the heart, enjoying life, seeking the deep and ordinary pleasures, eating in such a way that everyone is invited to your table—these are the soulful rules of conduct demonstrated in the Gospels.

His students asked him,
"When will the kingdom be here?"
Jesus answered, "It will not come by waiting
for it. It will not be a matter of saying, 'here it is'
or 'there it is.' No, the spirit of the father is spread
out on the earth and people don't see it."

—GOSPEL OF THOMAS 113–114

When spirituality moves too far from the body and the material world, it becomes joyless. That is because human pleasure almost always involves your own body and the bodies of others. I'm not referring only to sex but to gatherings of people, sport, play, dining, dancing, and traveling together. We are people of body, soul, and spirit, and Jesus' teaching addresses all three dimensions.

The father spirit is in this world, not as something alien but as something essential. The more you are alive in your body and enjoy the simple pleasures of life, the more grounded and joyful is your spirituality. The move downward into body is also a movement toward soul. The high spirit needs this downward connection or else it becomes overly aggressive and full of ego.

The kingdom is here and now. It isn't over there or on its way or entirely hidden. True, it is not apparent to ordinary eyes. Your eyes need to be washed with the holy water of metanoia. You need a change in vision to see the kingdom and participate in it. But it isn't essentially different from the world and the life you know.

The word *baptism* refers to dipping or immersing and could even apply to someone "deep" in trouble. But in Greek it was also used for dipping things in liquid to dye them. Dyeing is a good image for spiritual baptism as well, since when you are dipped into the imagination of the life Jesus offers, you change color. You're no longer the same person, and you don't see with the same eyes. Objectively, the world is the same as it has always been, but with your new perspective it looks entirely different.

This description is not mere wordplay. A Buddhist has to resolve a similar issue by grasping the paradox by which samsara (the wheel of everyday concerns) and nirvana (the state of having exited the frenetic life) are somehow identical. In the Jesus spirituality, ordinary life and the separate reality of the kingdom are in some sense the same.

The Gospels use strong words to describe Jesus' emotions. He was a full human being, even as his attention was focused on the kingdom of his father. The secret to Jesus' spirituality can be found in a short line from the Gospel of Thomas—"Split a piece of wood; I am there." The story of Krishna in India says something similar but from another point of view. He opens wide his mouth, and his mother looks in to see their entire universe. In our situation, you look at the universe and you see Jesus and his father.

The idea is not just to think abstractly about this paradox of Jesus and the material world, but, like him, to enjoy this life to the fullest as a path toward the father and a way into the kingdom. For Jesus was not recognized only as the one healing, teaching, and banishing the demonic. As at Emmaus, he revealed himself by means of his intellectual brilliance and a gesture at dinner—breaking bread in a spirit of conviviality.

We have yet to consider the wit and comic aspect of Jesus' stories, but add those qualities to his love of dining with friends and you sense a man who was immensely attractive and a joy to be around. You can turn these personal qualities into a theology, because Jesus was an archetypal figure as well as a historical one. He teaches through his actions and style as well as through his stories. To be his student means to live fully and to pay attention to the simple joys of life, to be the kind of person who makes friends and combines wit and sensuality.

Jesus' teachings suggest what many scholars call a "reversal" of values. To those people who think that being spiritual means to avoid life, deny yourself and others pleasure, judge someone else's lifestyle, recommend deprivation, and define goodness as austerity,

Jesus offers a profound reversal. No, he says clearly, don't hide from life in a cult of false virtue. Embrace life and enjoy it. Deep in that pleasure you will find the comfort and community that the father wishes for you.

CONCLUSION

The world is changing. When you look at the surface of cultural developments you see new technology, threats to the environment, and perhaps a loss of traditional religious piety. But if you look closer you may see deeper and more positive developments as well. More and more people are concerned about the planet on which we live, a sign of a maturing moral sense. We are slowly becoming less sexist and are even more open to men and women living the gay life, a sign that our own sexuality is less defensive. And many are passionate about moving past rote belief and obedience toward a more vibrant spiritual life. These changes can be confusing and challenging, but they also inspire hope.

These changes could allow us finally to appreciate what Jesus' teachings are all about. Today we are ready to read the Gospels and see the beauty and promise in Jesus' vision: not to create an exclusive group of chosen, lucky believers, but to glimpse an entire world able to summon up deep respect and even love, to create a global culture free of violence and the urge toward dominance.

Nothing in the Gospels suggests that Jesus was interested in creating a religion. He was offering everyone a chance for a peaceful and fulfilling life by adopting a different set of values. The crux, of course, is a shift from judgment, competition, and aggression to the rule of an open heart. The Gospels represent a movement out of narcissism and paranoia to a more mature, self-possessed life of deep community.

The Gospels do not focus on a plan for spiritual self-improvement and a virtuous personality. They are not a set of platitudes about living properly but rather a restructuring of the human imagination about how we can be in relation to each other and to the world. They offer a new way of imagining the human worldwide community.

How, then, do you live the Gospel spirit today? You do exactly what the Gospel says: Firstly, you cultivate a deep respect for people who are not of your circle and whom society rejects. I speak of respect rather than love, because love is too easily sentimentalized and because agape, as we saw in some detail, is about respect and affection rather than melodramatic emotion. Secondly, you do everything possible to deal effectively with demonic urges in yourself and in society. You do something about aggression, paranoia, narcissism, greed, jealousy, and violence. You live with a mindset that doesn't justify such things but seeks alternatives. Thirdly, you play the role of healer in every situation. The word *therapy* appears 47 times in the New Testament—you adopt a therapeutic posture in the style of Jesus the healer.[43] In all your work and interactions, you take the role of healer. Finally, you stay awake and don't fall into the unconsciousness of the age. You also help others wake up to a thoughtful life imagined in fresh, original, and convivial ways. In his last talk, Thomas Merton said, "First, one comes to a monastery to be cured; then, one prays for others or teaches them the cure."

These are the basics, and they have nothing to do with feeling virtuous or with what you believe and what happens to you in the afterlife. To deal with your mortality, you can live with faith, hope, doubt, and wonder, the building blocks of a spiritual life. Like Jesus in constant discourse with his cosmic father, you cooperate in your destiny, go beyond a materialistic life, do what you feel called to do, and let the flow of your existence take you where it will. Instead of worrying about the afterlife, you stand at the edge of your existence in hope and trust, responding creatively to the opportunities and challenges that come to you from the fatherly source of your existence.

Theologians have always said that Jesus is divine and human. He lived fully on this earth in the community of his friends and family, but he also never lost contact with his heavenly father. He was shamanic, skilled at being both earthy and visionary. He could be profoundly involved with his fellow humans and yet also metamorphose and be in the company of his visionary forebears.

European Renaissance theologians said that we, too, could be and should be both human and divine. *Deus humanus* was their phrase, a divine human. They saw what humans could accomplish in art and technology, and they had the strong spiritual imagination to see how we humans could take our part in the ongoing creation of the world: solving aggression, creating a world community, and cultivating a highly convivial life.

We have lost that spiritual vision and largely turned the Gospels into a book of moral standards. But now we have the opportunity to reread these documents with a renewed appreciation for the spiritual. We could recover that grand vision of the Renaissance and think more deeply about religion, spirituality, and Jesus' vision.

We could see in them an affirmation of the joy of human life and relationship. We could see a highly spiritual Jesus who is constantly aware of the father in heaven, and an Epicurean Jesus whose spirituality conflicts in no way with the sheer pleasures of bodily existence and human contact. We could appreciate the Jesus who cooks, dines, converses, enjoys an oil massage, and, in one passage at least, dances. We could emulate Jesus the poet, the one who sees everything as poetry, everything symbolic of deeper spiritual meaning.

Once you understand that the Gospels do not ask you to compete for the truth or swear allegiance to a creed or institution, you are free to study and think for yourself as you adopt the Jesus vision. You are neither fanatical nor lukewarm in your embrace of that intelligent and fascinating proposal for a new imagination of what human beings can do. There is indeed something saving about it: you can be saved from unconsciousness, meaninglessness, negativity and despair, depression, narcissism, and perfectionism.

In the last talk he ever gave, on his trip to Asia, Thomas Merton told a story about monks fleeing Tibet. A group made it out of the country and sent a message back to the others saying, "Now what do we do?" Their answer: "You're on your own." Merton applied that simple statement to monks today and, by implication, to all spiritual people. You have to assume responsibility for your spiritual life and not depend on the structures around you. You don't look for someone to give you rules; the further you go into life by taking on its challenges, you find the rules of your life and therefore its meaning and purpose.

You have to think for yourself and not carry the baggage of your religion. Most people seem to read the Gospels as a set of teachings and rules that demand a sacrifice of will and intellect. But Jesus encourages discussion and conviviality, a theme especially pronounced in the noncanonical Gospels, where his students discuss the teachings excitedly. He creates a community of strong individuals, not a collective of like-minded robots.

Life in the kingdom is like wine compared to water. It is an intensification and metamorphosis of ordinary life so that it becomes extraordinary. It is altruistic rather than narcissistic, welcoming of the other rather than paranoid. It is open to mystery, the spiritual, and the miraculous rather than enclosed in rationality and secularism.

The natural state is unconscious, lacking in imagination. The kingdom comes into being after metanoia, a deep shift in vision, understanding, and values. Anyone can, like Jesus, stand in the river of life's streaming and choose the new imagination of what it means to be a human. Anyone can decide to live rather than to hide. In making that choice, you exit the dead-end values of the age and enter the Gospel kingdom.

If you follow the example of Jesus and listen for your destiny and fate, you will have to go your own way, adapting the simple, radical, teachings to your own calling and circumstances. You will evoke the kingdom in your own style, making your own life a tiny mustard seed, cultivating the weeds of your thoughts, making yourself the embodiment of the moral beauty and spiritual intelligence found in the Gospels.

Acknowledgments

Writing this book has taken me back to my early 20s, when I lived in a religious community and was studying the Gospels as part of my training to be a priest. I never completed that training, but my life took a major turn because of those studies. My teacher then was a very young John Dominic Crossan. He inspired me to approach the Gospels with great care and intelligence. In this book I go in my own direction and in no way claim to represent Dr. Crossan's scholarship. As writers often say, my mistakes are my own. But I honor his continuing work for its skill and imagination.

I want to thank other friends who are Scripture scholars. George Nickelsburg, another imaginative writer and researcher, has encouraged me all along to write in an area where I am not an expert. Sister Wendy Cotter, too, a specialist in Gospel history and a valued friend, kept me writing when I had my doubts.

At home, conversations with Hari Kirin Kaur always sharpen my thoughts and send me off in new directions. It's a gift to live with someone who knows your work a little better than you do.

I am grateful to my agent Kim Witherspoon and her staff for seeing and appreciating what I am trying to do in my writing. I'm veering off toward greater eccentricity in my old age and am thankful for Kim's understanding. I could say the same about Patty Gift, my editor, and Reid Tracy of Hay House. They are giving me the chance to give voice to the many ideas and images stirring in me. I also thank Deborah Kory for her skillful help with the manuscript.

Finally I'd like to thank some writers I never met but whose daring work has influenced me in the area of the Gospels: Marcus Borg, Robert Funk, James Robinson, and Bernard Brandon Scott.

ENDNOTES

1. Oscar Wilde, "De Profundis," *The Complete Works of Oscar Wilde* (New York: Harper & Row, 1966), p. 933.

2. It is popular among some clergy and scholars to use alternative words for *basilea,* the Greek term—"domain" and "reign," for example. Some find "kingdom" sexist. When speaking directly of the Gospel texts, I prefer to use "kingdom" and otherwise "sphere," as in the spiritual sphere to which Jesus was so close.

3. Lao-tzu, *Tao Te Ching,* transl. Gia-Fu Feng and Jane English (New York: Vintage Books, 1972), no. 11.

4. Joseph Campbell, *The Masks of God: Creative Mythology* (New York: Viking Press, 1968), pp. 4–6.

5. For example, Eckhart is famous for having said: "The eye with which you see God is the eye with which God sees you."

6. The Greek root of "Gospel" is *euangelion* or "good message," perhaps even "good angel." The word was sometimes used in classical times for a good oracle.

7. I am not trying to paganize Gospel spirituality here but rather amplify and deepen the language and imagery used in the Gospels.

8. William Blake, "The Laocoön," in *The Complete Poetry and Prose of William Blake,* ed. David V. Erdman (Berkeley and Los Angeles: University of California Press, newly rev. ed., 1982), p. 273.

9. D. T. Suzuki, *An Introduction to Zen Buddhism* (New York: Grove Press, 1964), p. 88. Suzuki goes on to describe satori in language that could easily be applied to metanoia: "As satori strikes at the primary root of existence, its attainment generally marks a turning point in one's life. The attainment, however, must be thoroughgoing and clear-cut; a lukewarm satori, if there is such a thing, is worse than no satori."

10. Here you can see how the sacraments of baptism and confirmation in Christianity *could be* the occasions for profound developments

in a person and a community. But to have such an effect, the community would have to have a full and vital appreciation for ritual, something generally lacking in the modernist culture.

11. Charles W. Hedrick and Paul A. Mirecki, eds., *Gospel of the Savior* (n.p.: Polebridge Press, 1999), p. 41.

12. *The Gospel of Philip,* translation from the Coptic and commentary by Jean-Yves Leloup, transl. Joseph Rowe (Rochester, VT: Inner Traditions, 2003), p. 95.

13. Biblical scholars today refer to this mystery of eating together as "commensality." John Dominic Crossan says that for Jesus, "commensality was rather a strategy for building or rebuilding peasant community on radically different principles from those of honor and shame, patronage and clientage. It was based on an egalitarian sharing of spiritual and material power at the most grassroots level." *The Historical Jesus* (San Francisco: HarperSanFrancisco, 1992), p. 344.

14. Richard Seaford, *Dionysos* (London: Routledge, 2006), p. 121. "He [Dionysos] was said to have founded Scythopolis (in Hebrew named Beth-Shean, about 18 miles southeast of Nazareth), where evidence—mainly from the 2nd century A.D.—has been

WRITING IN THE SAND

unearthed for his cult. That the city was once known as Nysa, the place in myth where Dionysos was reared by the nymphs, is mentioned in the first century AD by Pliny the Elder."

15. Many of the Gospel stories and teachings do two things: They reiterate the central theme of the kingdom and of *metanoia*, a radical shift in vision. But they also offer a more specific idea about the kingdom and the nature of the shift. Cana has a Dionysian/Epicurean tone, even as it presents the basic image of transformation. Water to wine is metanoia but specifically a shift away from moralism toward the Dionysian and the Epicurean.

16. Ross King, *Michelangelo & the Pope's Ceiling* (New York: Penguin Books, 2003), p. 66.

17. John Howard Griffin, *Follow the Ecstasy: The Hermitage Years of Thomas Merton* (Maryknoll, NY: Orbis Books, 1993), p. 60.

18. *Essential Sufism,* James Fadiman and Robert Frager, eds. (Edison, NJ: Castle Books, 1997), p. 118.

19. Paul Murray, OP, "Drinking in the Word," http://www.op.org/global/sites/www.op.org/files/docs/en/Articles/murray_drinking.htm

20. For an elaboration on the Dionysian Jesus, see David L. Miller, *Christs: Meditations on Archetypal Images in Christian Theology* (New York: The Seabury Press, 1981), pp. 127–132.

21. See Crossan, *In Parables: The Challenge of the Historical Jesus* (Sonoma, CA: Polebridge Press, 1992), pp. 72–74. Crossan emphasizes the theme of reversal and the radical nature of the kingdom. Bernard Brandon Scott, on the other hand, leaves the parable more unresolved in *Re-Imagine the World: An Introduction to the Parables of Jesus* (Santa Rosa, CA: Polebridge Press, 2001), pp. 65–83.

22. Thomas Merton, *The Seven Storey Mountain* (New York: Harcourt Brace & Company, 1948), pp. 448–49.

23. Quoted in David Bromwich, "How Lincoln Won," *New York Review of Books* (September 19, 2006), p. 46.

24. Paul Tillich, *The Shaking of the Foundations* (New York: Charles Scribner's Sons, 1976), p. 162.

25. This reference to movies is not mere rhetoric. Popular theological thinking today is influenced by films about God and by those who have played him, from the mighty graybeard of *The Ten Commandments* to Morgan Freeman in *Bruce Almighty* and George Burns

in *Oh, God!* Certainly films like *The Exorcist* have placed thoughts about exorcism in the genre of horror.

26. We find many words to name the new life that Jesus represents, the life willed by the father. But it is always difficult to remember what it means—not a humanitarian, moral life, but one lived at an entirely different level of ethical and intellectual vision.

27. C. G. Jung, *Memories, Dreams, Reflections* ed. Aniela Jaffé, transl. Richard and Clara Winston (New York: Pantheon Books, 1973), pp. 170–199.

28. Jung says that psychologically the demonic can be recognized in its "ungovernable nature and overwhelming power." C. G. Jung, *Psychological Types, Collected Works* vol. 6, transl. R. F. C. Hull (Princeton, NJ: Princeton University Press, 1971), §347.

29. Joseph Epes Brown, ed., *The Sacred Pipe: Black Elk's Account of the Seven Rites of the Oglala Sioux* (Baltimore: Penguin Books, 1972), p. 14.

30. We can see this ideal in the long tradition of convivial monasteries and in the writings of Marsilio Ficino, who placed *convivium,* eating and talking with pleasure and seriousness, at the very heart of his philosophy.

31. The Irish writer John Moriarty sees this crossing of the "torrent" of Kedron as a highly significant act, a descent and a transition.

32. Pauline Moffitt Watts, *Nicolaus Cusanus: A Fifteenth-Century Vision of Man* (Leiden, the Netherlands: E. J. Brill, 1982), p. 108.

33. Teilhard de Chardin expresses a similar sentiment: "We are working for the fulfillment of the Pleroma by preparing its more or less near-to-our-hand material . . . victory over a narrow and lazy egoism." *The Divine Milieu* (New York: Harper Perennial, 2001), p. 62.

34. Oscar Wilde, *The Complete Works of Oscar Wilde* (New York: Harper Perennial, 1966), p. 1085.

35. Lao-tzu, *Tao Te Ching*. Transl. Gia-Fu Feng and Jane English (New York: Vintage Books, 1972), no. 49.

36. I treat all of these issues in my book *The Soul of Sex* (New York: HarperCollins, 1998).

37. Miranda Shaw, *Passionate Enlightenment: Women in Tantric Buddhism* (Princeton, NJ: Princeton University Press, 1994), p. 42.

38. Chögyam Trungpa, *Cutting Through Spiritual Materialism,* eds. John Baker and Marvin Casper (Boston: Shambhala, 1987), p. 13.

39. William Blake, "The Laocoön," in *The Complete Poetry and Prose of William Blake,* ed. David V. Erdman (Berkeley and Los Angeles: University of California Press, newly rev. ed., 1982), p. 722.

40. Oscar Wilde, *The Complete Works of Oscar Wilde* (New York: Harper Perennial, 1966), p. 931.

41. Ricky Alan Mayotte, *The Complete Jesus* (South Royalton, VT: Steerforth Press, 1998), pp. 145–148.

42. David Fideler, *Jesus Christ, Sun of God* (Wheaton, IL: Quest Books, 1993).

43. The use of "therapeutic" could be confusing. I don't mean it in the modern scientific sense where we use formal methods of cure and treatment. I mean it in the Socratic sense: service to the gods, service to the mysteries of life as they play out in people and in nature. You can have a healing (therapeutic) attitude in a marriage, toward your children, at work, in society.

About the Author

Best-selling author and psychotherapist **Thomas Moore** has written numerous books on spirituality, including *Soul Mates, Life at Work,* and the *New York Times* bestseller *Care of the Soul.* Born in Detroit, Michigan, to an Irish Catholic family, Thomas has devoted his life to the study of theology, world religions, Jungian and archetypal psychology, the history of art, and world mythology. He currently lives in New Hampshire.

NOTES

NOTES

NOTES

NOTES

NOTES

NOTES

NOTES

NOTES

NOTES

NOTES

Hay House Titles of Related Interest

YOU CAN HEAL YOUR LIFE, the movie,
starring Louise L. Hay & Friends
(available as a 1-DVD program and an expanded 2-DVD set)
Watch the trailer at: **www.LouiseHayMovie.com**

THE SHIFT, the movie,
starring Dr. Wayne W. Dyer
(available as a 1-DVD program and an expanded 2-DVD set)
Watch the trailer at: **www.DyerMovie.com**

◎◎◎

THE GOSPEL OF THE SECOND COMING:
Jesus is back . . . and this time he's funny!,
by Timothy Freke and Peter Gandy

LUCID LIVING: A Book You Can read in
One Hour That Will Turn Your World Inside Out,
by Timothy Freke

RETURN TO THE SACRED: Ancient Pathways to
Spiritual Awakening, by Jonathan Ellerby, Ph.D.

All of the above are available at your local bookstore,
or may be ordered by contacting Hay House (see last page).

We hope you enjoyed this Hay House book. If you'd like to receive a free catalog featuring additional Hay House books and products, or if you'd like information about the Hay Foundation, please contact:

Hay House, Inc.
P.O. Box 5100
Carlsbad, CA 92018-5100

(760) 431-7695 or (800) 654-5126
(760) 431-6948 (fax) or (800) 650-5115 (fax)
www.hayhouse.com® • www.hayfoundation.org

Published and distributed in Australia by: Hay House Australia Pty. Ltd., 18/36 Ralph St., Alexandria NSW 2015 • Phone: 612-9669-4299 • Fax: 612-9669-4144 • www.hayhouse.com.au

Published and distributed in the United Kingdom by: Hay House UK, Ltd., 292B Kensal Rd., London W10 5BE • Phone: 44-20-8962-1230 • Fax: 44-20-8962-1239 • www.hayhouse.co.uk

Published and distributed in the Republic of South Africa by: Hay House SA (Pty), Ltd., P.O. Box 990, Witkoppen 2068 • Phone/Fax: 27-11-467-8904 • orders@psdprom.co.za • www.hayhouse.co.za

Published in India by: Hay House Publishers India, Muskaan Complex, Plot No. 3, B-2, Vasant Kunj, New Delhi 110 070 • Phone: 91-11-4176-1620 • Fax: 91-11-4176-1630 • www.hayhouse.co.in

Distributed in Canada by: Raincoast, 9050 Shaughnessy St., Vancouver, B.C. V6P 6E5 • Phone: (604) 323-7100 Fax: (604) 323-2600 • www.raincoast.com

Tune in to **HayHouseRadio.com®** for the best in inspirational talk radio featuring top Hay House authors! And, sign up via the Hay House USA Website to receive the Hay House online newsletter and stay informed about what's going on with your favorite authors. You'll receive bimonthly announcements about Discounts and Offers, Special Events, Product Highlights, Free Excerpts, Giveaways, and more!
www.hayhouse.com®

HAY HOUSE

Tune in to Hay House Radio to listen to your favorite authors: **HayHouseRadio.com**®

Yes, I'd like to receive:
☐ **a Hay House catalog** ☐ *The Louise Hay Newsletter*
☐ *The Christiane Northrup Newsletter* ☐ *The Sylvia Browne Newsletter*

Name _____

Address _____

City _____ State _____ Zip _____

E-mail _____

Also, please send:
☐ **a Hay House catalog** ☐ *The Louise Hay Newsletter*
☐ *The Christiane Northrup Newsletter* ☐ *The Sylvia Browne Newsletter*

To:
Name _____

Address _____

City _____ State _____ Zip _____

E-mail _____

If you'd like to receive a catalog of Hay House books and products, or a free copy of one or more of our authors' newsletters, please visit **www.hayhouse.com**® or detach and mail this reply card.

To:

HAY HOUSE, INC.
P.O. Box 5100
Carlsbad, CA 92018-5100

Place
Stamp
Here